PENGUIN HANDBOOKS

FAST FOOD FOR VEGETARIANS

After training as a journalist, Janette Marshall worked on several regional newspapers before joining *Here's Health* where she was Assistant Editor for five years. She is particularly interested in nutrition and the role diet has to play in preventing and curing illness and in health problems. She has already written several books including *Slim Naturally*, *High-Fibre Cooking*, *The Wholefood Cookery Course*, *The Alternative Chocolate Book* and *Shopping for Health* which was published in Penguin in 1987.

FAST FOOD
FOR VEGETARIANS

For Busy, Healthy Eaters

Janette Marshall

PENGUIN BOOKS

Penguin Books Ltd, 27 Wrights Lane, London W8 5TZ (Publishing and Editorial)
and Harmondsworth, Middlesex, England (Distribution and Warehouse)
Viking Penguin Inc., 40 West 23rd Street, New York, New York 10010, USA
Penguin Books Australia Ltd, Ringwood, Victoria, Australia
Penguin Books Canada Ltd, 2801 John Street, Markham, Ontario, Canada L3R 1B4
Penguin Books (NZ) Ltd, 182–190 Wairau Road, Auckland 10, New Zealand

First published 1987

Made and printed in Great Britain by
Cox and Wyman Ltd, Reading, Berks
Filmset in Sabon (Linotron 202) by
Rowland Phototypesetting Ltd
Bury St Edmunds, Suffolk

CONTENTS

INTRODUCTION

Take two minutes to ask yourself the following questions: Are you a busy person who wants to arrive home from work and have something to eat on the table as quickly as possible? Would you also like that quick meal to be relatively 'healthy' and use unrefined foods but without the fuss of soaking beans, boiling pulses and taking a lot of trouble? Would you prefer to be doing things other than slaving over the stove or standing at work in the kitchen – unless it's cooking to entertain your friends at a more leisurely pace? Would you also like the added bonus of *vegetarian* meals that are realistically achievable in a short time?

If the answer to any of these questions is yes, then *Fast Food for Vegetarians* can help you solve your meatless meal problems without reaching, yet again, for the baked beans. It offers quick and easy recipes that can be made after a busy day at work, recipes for weekend entertaining – when you have more time – and ideas for vegetarian lunchboxes. You will also find tips for equipping the vegetarian kitchen and guidance on how to stock a vegetarian larder, freezer and fridge that incorporates practical choices for healthy eating.

PART ONE

Planning a Practical Vegetarian Lifestyle

BEING A VEGETARIAN
(or Vegan)

SWAPPING LIFESTYLES

There are many reasons why you or your guests, family and friends might prefer to have meatless meals. You may be concerned about the ethical considerations of eating meat and about the exploitation of animals. Perhaps your religion forbids meat or it may be that reasons of taste have led you to choose vegetarian foods.

A recent Gallup poll commissioned by Realeat, the makers of Vege Burgers, suggested that for about three million vegetarians in Britain the main reason for giving up, or cutting down on, meat was health. Concern about meat being high in fat or containing residues of drugs used in modern farming techniques may have been at the back of the interviewees' minds. Certainly current studies are proving that vegetarians are slimmer than meat-eaters, and that they have lower blood cholesterol levels, lessening their risk of heart disease. Other research has shown that vegetarians are less likely to suffer from gallstones and diverticulitis. Long-term studies are now investigating whether there is less breast cancer among vegetarian women and less heart and bowel disease (including cancer of the colon) among male and female vegetarians.

But if you don't eat meat what can you eat? Vegetarians give up meat and fish (although a surprising number of people who call themselves vegetarians continue to eat fish) but they do eat dairy produce such as eggs, milk, cheese, cream, yoghurt and butter. The term lacto-vegetarian is sometimes used to describe this pattern of eating.

Vegans go further and give up all animal produce – as well as not eating meat and fish, neither do they eat dairy produce. Sometimes people describing themselves as strict vegetarians eat an almost vegan diet. So it's a good idea to ask your vegetarian guests well in advance of a visit exactly what they don't eat. It's also sensible to ask any visitors you don't know well the same question!

REPLACING MEAT

Having given up meat, you obviously then don't want to spend your time finding processed or canned foods and soya products that mimic meat – unless of course you're trying to give up meat but still hanker after it. The majority of vegetarians don't want to be given meat-flavoured TVP or canned soya sausages and 'meat' balls.

So what can you eat or give your guests to replace the nutrients obtained from meat? The main concern of most people who have to cater for others is giving them enough protein. In fact this is probably the area where you have least to worry about as there is plenty of protein in the vegetarian diet.

The first thing you can do is to forget the categories of first-class proteins for animal foods and second-class protein for plant foods. These terms were coined around the time of the First World War when nutrition was still a new science. The distinction has since been seen to be unsound and also unfair to plants! It's true that there is a difference in the proportions of amino-acids found in plant and animal foods, but this is not a problem. Amino-acids are the building blocks your body needs to make protein from. There are twenty-one, and of these eight cannot be made in the body so you have to eat them in food. In meat, fish and the protein in dairy foods and eggs, the eight amino-acids are in the right proportion for your needs. In plants such as vegetables and cereals they are not, but by matching two of the three groups of plant protein foods you can make up for deficiencies in one group with the larger amounts in another group and so put together a jigsaw that makes complete protein.

MAKING COMPLETE PROTEIN

The three groups of plant foods are:

Grains	Legumes	Nuts and Seeds
barley	Beans:	almond
buckwheat	adzuki	brazil
bulgur	borlotti	cashew
couscous	black-eye	chestnut
maize	butter	coconut
millet	cannellini	hazelnut
oats	flageolet	peanut

Grains	Legumes	Nuts and Seeds
rye	*Beans:*	pecan
rice	field	pistachio
	haricot (baked)	walnut
	or navy	
	kidney	
	lima	
	mung	
	navy	
	lentils	
	chickpeas	

The best combinations are meals that contain legumes and nuts or seeds or those meals made up with legumes and grains. It's thought that the groups should be combined at the same meal – they can't provide complete protein if, for example, you have toast for breakfast and beans for lunch.

Legumes and Nuts or Seeds	Legumes and Grains
hummus	baked beans on toast
nut and seed salads	bean/chickpea 'curries' and
bean burgers coated in sesame	rice/breads
seeds	hummus and pitta bread
salads with beans and sunflower	tahini and wholemeal bread
seeds	tacos and refried beans
sprouted bean and seed stir-fries	pasta and bean salads (and soups)
and salads	peanut butter sandwiches
nut roasts with added seeds	
muffins, biscuits or cakes with	
nuts and seeds	

If some of the above foods are unfamiliar to you, look them up in 'The Vegetarian Larder' p. 35.

Eating dairy produce with one or more of the vegetable, protein group foods will further enhance the protein value.

OMELETTES AREN'T ENOUGH

If you are a lacto-vegetarian who eats dairy produce there may be a temptation to rely rather a lot on cheese and eggs because they are easy, convenient and complete. The disadvantage of doing so is not only a lack of variety in your diet – missing the opportunity of enjoying many other foods – but also that you wouldn't benefit from some of the major advantages of a vegetarian diet.

The two real bonuses of vegetable protein are that it contains fibre and it is low in fat. Replacing one high-fat, fibre-free food (meat) with another high-fat fibre-free food (cheese or eggs) is not the answer. One present study shows that many vegetarians have just as high a fat intake as their meat-eating peers. This has surprised researchers on the Oxford ten-year study (1980–90) because they had thought that vegetarians would have a lower fat intake than the average Briton's 40 per cent of calories. Cutting down on meat has been one of the actions suggested by NACNE (National Advisory Committee on Nutrition Education) health experts as a way to reduce fat consumption to 30–35 per cent of our calorie intake. NACNE and COMA (Committee on Medical Aspects/Food Policy) recommend this reduction in meat-eating in their Report on Diet and Cardiovascular Disease to help lessen the risk of heart disease and to keep slim. Cutting down on fat (whether saturated or unsaturated) helps slimmers because fat has more calories per gram than carbohydrates or protein.

GOING HI-FI

NACNE has also recommended increasing our fibre intake because fibre helps to bulk and soften waste as it passes through the gut. This gets it out of the system quicker and so prevents constipation. Speedy transit time means there is less chance of toxins being reabsorbed from the large bowel, and avoiding constipation also reduces the risk of diverticulitis and the possibility of varicose veins.

Soluble fibre (see also p. 14) also binds with unwanted excess fats like cholesterol and transports them away from arteries where they can form plaque and so increase heart-attack risks. It can also help prevent excess cholesterol in the bloodstream which may otherwise form gallstones.

BRING ON THE WHOLEFOODS

There are various ways you can add fibre to your vegetarian diet and many vegetarians base their vegetable proteins on whole grains and cereals. So when you have beans on toast, taking the wholefood approach means making the toast wholemeal. Similarly you get more vitamins, minerals and fibre if you change from white pasta to wholemeal pasta and from polished, white rice to brown rice. Eating brown rice may also result in fewer duodenal ulcers, common in populations whose staple food is white rice. By making more use of whole grains, you will automatically have fewer cheese- and egg-based meals on the menu. And as you will see from the store-cupboard items and recipes that doesn't mean spending an inordinate amount of time soaking and boiling beans.

Reducing your use of cheese and eggs – it's suggested by some experts that four eggs a week should be the most you eat, unless you are already on a low-fat and high-fibre diet – will also cut down on fat in the diet, which, as you will see below, most of us need to do. Added to the fact that you have already given up, or cut down on, meat, it should mean that you are reducing the amount of saturated fat you eat. And this is another advantage of the wholefood/vegetarian approach. Generally speaking, saturated fats in your diet come from animal foods, and when NACNE tell you to cut down on fat, they particularly mention saturated fats, as do the COMA nutritionists.

OILING THE WORKS

By cutting down on saturated fats, the ratio of polyunsaturated to saturated fats in the diet should automatically change for the better. By choosing a vegetarian wholefood way of eating, you are improving your fat balance by replacing hard, animal cooking fats like lard and suet (and even butter in some cases) with vegetable alternatives.

You do have to be a little careful because it's not simply a case of switching to any vegetable fat. There are some hard, vegetable cooking fats that are as saturated as animal fats. Another general rule on fat is that the harder it is, the more saturated it is. Food manufacturers can start off with a liquid vegetable oil or soft vegetable fat and turn it into a hard vegetable block of cooking fat, using the process of hydrogenation. This adds hydrogen to the molecules of polyunsaturated, unsaturated or monounsaturated fats and saturates them. Being saturated, they become hard and are no longer volatile, liquid unsaturated fats. Saturated vegetable and hydrogenated vegetable fats are thought to be as harmful to the body as saturated animal fats.

So, if you give up butter because it's high in saturates, you could swap it for a soft vegetable margarine that is 'high in polyunsaturates'. For cooking, you might choose a vegetable oil such as corn oil or soya oil. These two are more stable at high temperatures than sunflower and safflower, which are therefore better for salad dressings or cold use.

Making these changes will alter the ratio of saturated to poly-unsaturated fats in the diet. The COMA Report on Diet and Cardiovascular Disease recommended aiming for a ratio of 0.45:1 polyunsaturated to saturated, but some experts say we need to aim for 1:1 if we want to lower high blood-fat profiles and so reduce the risk of coronary heart disease.

Olive oil is a monounsaturated oil, at neither extreme of the saturated or polyunsaturated scale. It has been suggested that traditional Mediterranean food does not lead to heart disease because, complementing other healthy aspects of the diet, the oil used is monounsaturated olive oil. Monounsaturates do not add to the risk of heart disease as saturated fats do. Whether they lessen the risk of heart disease by 'scavenging' and removing some potentially problematic saturated fats as polyunsaturates is being investigated.

Finally, one more point on oils: there are two in particular, coconut and palm, that are highly saturated despite their being vegetable in origin.

NO BONES ABOUT IT

Having thought about their high fat content, you have now probably cut down on the amount of eggs you use, the number of meals you base on hard cheese (and you've probably stopped nibbling cheese and started to respect it more as a high calorie food) and you may have swapped full-fat milk for semi-skimmed or skimmed. (Inciden-tally, skimmed and semi-skimmed milk have as much, or more, calcium than full-fat milk because the calcium is not in the fatty part of the milk lost in skimming.) You may even have gone further and cut out dairy foods – if you've been attracted to veganism – and use soya milk instead of cows', goats' or sheep's milk.

If you've switched to goats' or sheep's milk, it is higher in fat than cows' milk. It may not appear to be so because there's no visible layer of cream that rises to the top. This is because goats' and sheep's milk are naturally homogenized – the particles of fat are spread evenly throughout the milk, are smaller and lighter, and don't separate out. Many people find homogenized milk easier to digest and an added bonus is that the proteins in these milks don't seem to produce as many allergic· reactions or sensitivities, causing skin problems or asthmatic conditions and their symptoms, as cows' milk can.

If you have become vegan, then you may be wondering where the calcium for bones and teeth and for the many functions in the body is going to come from now you don't drink milk or eat cheese and eggs. Whole grains contain useful amounts and you will now be eating more of these. Cereals, muesli and oatmeal will contribute some calcium too. Beans and other pulses, nuts and seeds (tahini), dark green vegetables and dried fruit, especially figs, also add calcium. White bread is still fortified with calcium, so it contains more than wholemeal bread, but wholemeal is nonetheless a very useful source in a wholefood diet. White flour that is unfortified will contain only half the amount of calcium in wholemeal flour.

The ability to use calcium in the body is affected by many factors. Ways in which you can enhance absorption are: make sure you also get enough vitamin D and magnesium and avoid taking raw bran or too much oxalic acid in chocolate, rhubarb and other fruit and vegetables. Calcium absorption can also be prevented if too much phosphorus in the form of phosphates is eaten, so watch out for phosphate food additives (the E450 series), or better still avoid the kind of processed and 'junk' foods that contain these. Nuts are also high in phosphorus, but you will use these sparingly because they have a high oil, and therefore calorie, content and because they are expensive! A high protein diet is generally high in phosphorus.

A diet high in saturated fat also makes it difficult for the body to use calcium. If you're an expectant mother your calcium needs will increase to build the bones of your baby and when you breastfeed you will also be supplying your baby with calcium. Growing children and teenagers have high calcium needs and the elderly should have extra calcium too, because their losses are greater and their absorption capacity deteriorates. In women the change in hormone output after the menopause encourages calcium losses from bones, so stock up when you're young. The losses can add up to about 1lb/450g or more over twenty to thirty years, and can lead to osteoporosis (demineralization of bones) and the all-too-common fractured and broken bones of old age. A milky, bedtime drink can help reduce some overnight calcium loss in the elderly, but it is better to ensure an adequate store in youth with good diet and exercise – which also builds healthy bones. You might have seen claims by the sweet industry that chocolate, or cocoa powder to be precise, is a good source of calcium and iron. This approach might suit the sweet industry because we would have to eat a large amount of their products, but it is *not* a good idea for our diet. Their claims fail to take into account the large amounts of oxalic acid in chocolate which inhibit absorption of calcium and may be the link between spotty skins and chocolate! Calcium is needed for zinc to be used and zinc is essential for a healthy skin.

PUMPING IRON

Although Popeye did much to raise awareness of the need for iron, he never got round to explaining that the iron in his spinach was different from the iron in meat. Perhaps no one ever told him that the iron in its non-haem form in spinach is not as readily available to the body as the haem form in meat and fish. Non-haem iron in vegetable foods has to be reduced to a different form and vitamin C is essential – otherwise vegetarian iron won't get across the intestinal wall and into the blood where it's needed.

Other foods can also affect absorption of vegetarian iron. Phytic acid, mainly problematic in raw bran, immobilizes iron and so do the foods high in phosphates (which also interfere with calcium). Even the tannic acid in a cup of tea can stop iron being absorbed and some medical experts have linked the British addiction to a 'cuppa' with poor iron levels and high incidence of anaemia.

Women vegetarians and vegans who are menstruating, expecting babies and breastfeeding need to pay particular attention to iron intake. Good food sources are dark greens, dried fruits, nuts, whole grains, beans, soya flour, oatmeal and wholemeal bread and flour. Remember that eating these foods with vitamin-C-rich foods, citrus fruits or juice enhances absorption.

THAT ZINCING FEELING

While you might not feel ill, you could feel a lot better if you had an adequate intake of zinc, argue researchers, looking at the importance of zinc in our diet. As the main source of zinc is meat, vegetarians and vegans may be going short. Zinc from meat is also more readily available to the body than vegetarian sources of the mineral, which include brewer's yeast, cheese and eggs, carrots, peanuts, green beans, tomatoes, peas, potatoes and sweetcorn. Wholegrain cereals, such as brown rice and wholemeal and rye bread, and breakfast cereals also provide some zinc. Like iron, vegetarian sources of zinc are more readily available to the body if eaten with food rich in vitamin C. Phytic acid may interfere with absorption and so may TVP-textured vegetable protein, which is high in phytate. Prospective parents, expectant and breastfeeding mothers need extra zinc as the mineral is vital for healthy reproduction.

VITAMIN B_{12}

This is another of those nutrients vital for health and obtained by most people from meat, fish and to a lesser extent in cheese. The liver can store vitamin B_{12} for some years, but supplies will eventually run out. Live yoghurt is a good source because B_{12} is produced by bacteria which turn milk into yoghurt. They will be present in all yoghurts except those that have been pasteurized or heat-treated in other ways to make long-life, sterile yoghurt. Calcium is also needed for the body to use B_{12}, so yoghurt is an excellent food for vegetarians – as well as being versatile and tasty! Apart from these animal foods, B_{12} occurs only in one plant food, a kind of algae called spirulina which is dried and made into tablets sold in health-food shops.

B_{12} is also cultured on plant materials to make vegetarian vitamin B_{12} tablets or to provide a vegetarian's source of the vitamin which can be used to enrich some brands of soya milk, some yeast extracts and some soya foods. Read their labels, ingredients listings and packages to see which contain B_{12} (see also 'The Vegetarian Larder' p. 35). Again, pregnant women have special needs for vitamin B_{12} and so do the elderly. Alcohol and smoking deplete body stores of this vitamin, as they do of most vitamins and minerals.

THE SUNSHINE VITAMIN

This is another name for vitamin D, so called because it can be made by the skin as a result of exposure to the sun. It is needed by the body so that you can use calcium. Most people get vitamin D in their diet from butter and margarine (along with vitamin A) but many margarines contain whey (milk product) or other milk products, so strict vegetarians and vegans prefer brands of margarine that are free from animal products and also contain vitamin D.

EYES RIGHT

You were probably told, as a child, to eat up your carrots so you could see in the dark – and vitamin A deficiency can lead to night blindness. Vitamin A is found only in animal foods such as cod liver oil, liver, cheese, eggs and butter. Margarines are fortified with vitamins A and D to bring them up to the level of butter. Fortunately, for vegans and vegetarians, coloured pigments in orange and green vegetables and fruit (carotenoids) are precursors of vitamin A. This means they are not vitamins in their own right but are converted to Vitamin A in the intestine and liver. Dark green vegetables, sweet potatoes, pumpkins, apricots and peaches are all good sources of carotenoids.

THE BALANCED DIET

Your special requirements as a vegan or vegetarian don't override the general healthy eating guidelines that have been suggested by the NACNE and COMA reports. You will probably find that by putting wholefood vegetarian or vegan principles into practice you will have a good diet, but nevertheless it is worth looking at the composition of the average British diet and considering what these health experts suggest to help you get the balance right. In fact, many people think you could do even better than the goals set for the general population to reach by the 1990s – but one step at a time . . .

The basic changes suggested by NACNE are outlined below:
- reduce the amount of fat you eat by a quarter
- reduce the amount of sugar you eat by a half

- reduce the amount of salt you eat by a quarter
- increase the amount of fibre you eat by a half.

Fat

At the moment fat accounts for 38–40 per cent of our calorie intake. If you intend to cut it down, then for vegetarians the foods to watch out for are: high fat hard cheeses, butter and margarine, cooking oils and fats, salad creams and dressings, cream, pastry, cakes, biscuits, nuts – especially those high in saturated fats such as cashews.

Sugar

We eat about 100lb/45.5kg of sugar a year. Like fat, some of it is visible as sugar added to drinks and sprinkled on breakfast cereal and fruit. Some is invisible and has been incorporated into processed foods such as sauces and even savoury foods where you might not expect to find it. The foods to watch out for are: processed foods, canned foods, breakfast cereals, cakes, biscuits, pastries, pies, desserts, sauces, packet desserts, fruit drinks, coffee creamers and whiteners, sweets, chocolates, jam, marmalade, honey, treacle, etc.

It is a myth that you need sugar from the packet for energy or that when you flag you should grab a bar of chocolate confectionery. These are the kinds of food that make you feel tired and tend to make you crave more sugary snacks. Better sources of energy are starchy foods or unrefined carbohydrate foods such as wholemeal bread and pasta, potatoes and other root vegetables. Because they are high in fibre they give you a slow and sustained release of energy that avoids the peaks and troughs of the sugar addict's cycle.

Salt

The average British intake of salt is about 12g/½oz a day and that's more than enough. You would be better to be nearer 3g/⅑oz a day, and you don't even *need* that much. All the sodium we need for a healthy diet is naturally present in fruit, vegetables, whole grains, cheese, milk, etc. Cutting down will reduce the risk of high blood pressure and also of strokes and heart disease.

If you are trying to cut down salt, the most obvious thing to do is to stop using the salt cellar and gradually reduce the amount you add to food during cooking. It's just a question of taste and you can wean yourself off salt. Other places to watch out for salt are smoked and salted foods, foods in brine and other preserved foods. Salt is also added to most processed and baked foods and it is found even in sweet foods. Breakfast cereals, canned foods, packet foods and soup mixes will also contain salt – sodium is the base for many food additives – so watch out for these on food ingredients listings either by name or get to know your sodium E numbers.

Fibre

We've seen that switching to unrefined carbohydrates is the way to increase fibre intake and that means using wholemeal and other wholegrain breads, wholemeal flour, wholemeal pasta, brown rice and other grains. Fresh fruit and vegetables also add fibre to the diet.

Eating more of these foods is preferable to choosing white, refined carbohydrate foods and sprinkling bran on them. This is not just a question of taste – bran is pretty unpalatable stuff – but also because raw bran is high in phytic acid and phytates can interfere with mineral absorption. However, it is thought that the phytic acid and phytates naturally present in wholemeal products are not harmful because they are either destroyed by processing (of bread and yeast doughs) or the high temperatures of baking. It has also been seen that the body adjusts to the phytates present in a wholefood diet and so does not fail to absorb all the extra minerals provided by these foods.

Apart from cereal foods, fibre is also present in beans and pulses which have, in common with oats, a good deal of soluble fibre. This is a gummy fibre whose properties help control the cholesterol in our blood and prevent it from being deposited as arterial plaque, so reducing the risk of heart disease. The gummy nature of soluble fibre also helps give a slow release of energy (like insoluble cereal fibre) and it may also inhibit cholesterol deposits which cause gallstones.

Diabetic vegetarians and vegans could be helped by soluble fibre because it seems to help regulate blood-sugar levels and, like other unrefined carbohydrates, avoids sudden demands on the pancreas for insulin. Low-fibre foods make these demands because they are sugary and digested very quickly, flooding the blood with sugar.

One final word on high-fibre foods. Don't be conned by some of the breakfast cereals and bakery goods that claim to be 'high in fibre' or 'wholemeal'. They may well also be very high in fat and sugar to make the bran they contain palatable. The best way to get your fibre is from naturally occurring fibre in unrefined foods. Otherwise you may end up paying quite a lot for high-fibre foods that are not really very 'healthy'.

DAY BY DAY

There are many options open to both vegetarians and vegans for varying the daily diet. Even though you have excluded some foods, there are still a lot to choose from. The main thing is to keep variety going throughout the day. For example, if you have toast or bread for breakfast, have something other than sandwiches for lunch or pizza for dinner. Mixing and matching makes more exciting meals and draws on a wider range of foods, each with its own vitamin and mineral combinations.

If you have a criteria listing for improving your diet, then you might like to put fats at the top of this list and try to keep to below 3oz/75g a day – this figure includes visible and invisible fats. Although the list below shows three meals a day, there's no special need to eat that number. You might find that snacking (or grazing, as Americans call it) through the day suits you better – as long as you don't over-eat or eat too little. Similarly, your main meal could be either at midday or in the evening. Or you may prefer just two meals a day and eat fruit and vegetables as the rest of your intake.

TYPICAL DAY'S EATING

Breakfasts

<u>Vegan</u>
wholemeal toast or bread, vegan margarine
preserves (no-added-sugar), peanut butter, tahini, yeast extract
muesli – oats, dried fruit, nuts, fresh fruit, soya milk or fruit juice
porridge – rolled oats, oatmeal, oatbran and oatgerm
dried fruit compote
wheatgerm

fresh fruit
soya milk yoghurt
baked beans
mushrooms
muffins
waffles
pancakes
wholemeal croissants
breakfast cereals – no-added-sugar and salt varieties include
    Shredded Wheat, Cubs, Puffed Wheat

Vegetarian

The vegan menu plus these extras:
free-range eggs – poached, boiled or scrambled with minimum fat
    and salt
crispbreads and cheese
yoghurt
honey
butter and polyunsaturated margarine
skimmed milk, or goats' or sheep's milk

To drink

decaffeinated coffee or coffee substitutes
herb teas or low-tannin teas such as Luaka, St James's brands
mineral water, still or sparkling
fresh fruit and vegetable juices
carob soya milk drinks or carob with standard milks
soya milk

Lunch

Vegan

wholemeal or other wholegrain pitta, crispbread and open sand-
    wiches, filled or topped with salad, nut butters and spreads such as
    tahini, sunflower spread, vegan pâtés, hummus
salads, fresh vegetable and fruit, plus nuts, beans and other grains
vegan pasties and quiches
pizzas with vegetable toppings

Vegetarian

The vegan menu plus these extras:
egg and cheese sandwich fillings
egg and cheese salads
pizzas with cheese toppings
wholemeal quiches
vegetarian burgers, rissoles and scotch eggs

Evening meal

You can, of course, have anything from the lunch suggestions for an evening meal, or vice versa.

Vegan

vegetable, nut-, pasta- or miso- (fermented soya bean paste) based soups
vegetables stuffed with rice or other grains and nuts
homemade or packet vegan burgers, pasties, rissoles
wholemeal vegetable crumbles, pies and gratins
tofu burgers, dips, quiches, stir-fries
seitan (wheat gluten) baked Chinese or Japanese dishes
nut roasts and loaves
risottos with beans and nuts
vegetable and bean casseroles
wholemeal pancakes with different fillings
wholemeal pasta and sauces
ethnic vegan dishes

Vegetarian

The vegan menu plus these extras:
pastries, pancakes and gratins using cheese
soufflés, omelettes, egg-based quiches, eggs *en cocotte*
cheese and grain burgers, roast loaves, quiches
cheese dips and pâtés
gougères with vegetable fillings

Desserts

Vegan

fresh fruit, fresh fruit salads, stewed fruit, dried fruit compotes

jellies and blancmanges made with vegetable setting-agents such as agar agar and soya milk
mousses, using soya milk and agar agar or tofu
tofu-based 'cheesecakes' and 'cream' desserts
wholemeal fruit pies and crumbles, crêpes and pancakes
gâteaux without eggs
soya-based yoghurts, frozen desserts
sorbets

Vegetarian

The vegan menu plus these extras:
dairy-based soufflés and mousses set with agar agar
gâteaux using eggs, wholemeal flour and yoghurt 'cream'
cheesecakes with low-fat cheeses and yoghurt
choux pastry desserts
sorbets and ice-creams
yoghurt
steamed puddings

Alcohol

Vegetarians and vegans who drink wine and beer will probably want to check that their favourite drink is free from animal ingredients or additives. The Vegetarian Society and the Vegan Society keep members informed on this score (see 'Useful Addresses' p. 212), or you could ask the manufacturer.

Food additives

You will probably want to avoid unnecessary additives where possible because they often indicate processed or refined foods. However, not all additives are 'bad' and some may be beneficial nutrients – vitamins used to enrich food or Vitamin E which acts as an antioxidant, for example. More pertinent to your needs as a vegetarian or vegan is the knowledge of whether a food additive is animal, vegetable or mineral in origin. The following table will give you this information.

TABLE 1

Food Additives: *Their Sources*

Note: if there is more than one entry it means that the additive may be from either of the sources entered. If the exact source is not stated on the label, you could check it with the manufacturer.

A   animal – derived from animal source
V   vegetarian – animal-free, but may derive from dairy produce
V   vegan – totally animal free
M   mineral – may be vitamin or mineral, naturally occurring or synthesized, or may be totally synthetic

		Animal	Vegetarian	Vegan	Mineral
Colours					
E100	Curcumin				
E101	Riboflavin (Lactoflavin)		V	V	
101(a)	Riboflavin-5′-phosphate				M
E102	Tartrazine				M
E104	Quinoline Yellow				M
107	Yellow 2G				M
E110	Sunset Yellow FCF (Orange Yellow S)				M
E120	Cochineal (Carmine of Cochineal or Carminic acid)	A			
E122	Carmoisine (Azorubine)				M
E123	Amaranth				M
E124	Ponceau 4R (Cochineal Red A)				M
E127	Erythrosine BS				M
128	Red 2G				M
E131	Patent Blue V				M

		Animal	Vegetarian	Vegan	Mineral
E132	Indigo Carmine (Indigotine)				M
133	Brilliant Blue FCF				M
E140	Chlorophyll		V	✓	
E141	Copper complexes of chlorophyll and chlorophyllins		V	✓	
E142	Green S (Acid Brilliant Green BS or Lissamine Green)				M
E150	Caramel		V	✓	
E151	Black PN (Brilliant Black BN)				M
E153	Carbon Black (Vegetable Carbon)	A	V	✓	M
154	Brown FK				M
155	Brown HT (Chocolate Brown HT)				M
E160(a)	Alpha-carotene, beta-carotene, gamma-carotene		V	✓	M
E160(b)	Annato, bixin, norbixin		V	✓	
E160(c)	Capsanthin (Capsorubin)		V	✓	
E160(d)	Lycopene		V	✓	
E160(e)	Beta-apo-8'-carotenal (C_{30})		V	✓	M
E160(f)	Ethyl ester of beta-apo-8'-cartenoic acid (C_{30})		V	✓	
E161(a)	Flavoxanthin		V	✓	M
E161(b)	Lutein		V	✓	
E161(c)	Cryptoxanthin		V	✓	
E161(d)	Rubixanthin		V	✓	
E161(e)	Violaxanthin		V	✓	
E161(f)	Rhodoxanthin		V	✓	
E161(g)	Canthaxanthin	A	V	✓	

E162	Beetroot Red (Betanin)		V		
E163	Anthocyanins		V	V	
E170	Calcium carbonate				M
E171	Titanium dioxide				M
E172	Iron oxides, iron hydroxides				M
E173	Aluminium				M
E174	Silver				M
E175	Gold				M
E180	Pigment Rubine (Lithol Rubine BK)				M

Preservatives

E200	Sorbic acid		V		M
E201	Sodium sorbate		V	V	M
E202	Potassium sorbate				M
E203	Calcium sorbate	A			M
E210	Benzoic acid				M
E211	Sodium benzoate				M
E212	Potassium benzoate				M
E213	Calcium benzoate	A			M
E214	Ethyl 4-hydroxybenzoate (Ethyl *para*-hydroxybenzoate)				M
E215	Etnyl 4-hydroxybenzoate, sodium salt (Sodium ethyl *para*-hydroxybenzoate)		Benzonic acid and its derivatives occur naturally in some fruits, but produced synthetically as a food additive		M
E216	Propyl 4-hydroxybenzoate (Propyl *para*-hydroxybenzoate)				M

	Animal	Vegetarian	Vegan	Mineral
E217	Propyl 4-hydroxybenzoate, sodium salt (Sodium propyl *para*-hydroxybenzoate)			M
E218	Methyl 4-hydroxybenzoate (Methyl *para*-hydroxybenzoate)			M
E219	Methyl 4-hydroxybenzoate, sodium salt (Sodium methyl *para*-hydroxybenzoate)			
E220	Sulphur dioxide			M
E221	Sodium sulphite			M
E222	Sodium hydrogen sulphite (Sodium bisulphite)			M
E223	Sodium metabisulphite			M
E224	Potassium metabisulphite			M
E226	Calcium sulphite			M
E227	Calcium hydrogen sulphite (Calcium bisulphite)	A		M
E230	Bipheny (Diphenyl)			M
E231	2-Hydroxybiphenyl (Orthophenylphenol)			M
E232	Sodium biphenyl-2-yl oxide (Sodium orthophenylphenate)			M
E233	2-(Thiazol-4-yl) benzimidazole (Thiabendazole)			M
234	Nisin	A		M

	Animal	Vegetarian	Vegan	Mineral
E236	Formic acid not }	A	V		M
E237	Sodium formate permitted }	A	V	V	M
E238	Calcium formate in the UK }	A	V	V	M
E239	Hexamine (Hexamethylenetetramine)				
E249	Potassium nitrite				M
E250	Sodium nitrite				M
E251	Sodium nitrate				M
E252	Potassium nitrate				M
E260	Acetic acid				M
E261	Potassium acetate				M
E262	Sodium hydrogen diacetate				M
262	Sodium acetate e				M
E263	Calcium acetate	A	V		M
E270	Lactic acid	A			M
E280	Propionic acid				M
E281	Sodium propionate				M
E282	Calcium propionate	A			M
E283	Potassium propionate				M
E290	Carbon dioxide		V	V	M
296	DL-malic acid, L-malic acid	V-L form	V-L form	√-L form	√DL form
297	Fumaric acid	A	V	√	M

Antioxidants		Animal	Vegetarian	Vegan	Mineral	
E300	L-ascorbic acid		V	V	M	}
E301	Sodium L-ascorbate			V	M	} Vitamin C
E302	Calcium L-ascorbate	A			M	}

	Animal	Vegetarian	Vegan	Mineral	
E304	6-O-palmitoyl-L-ascorbic acid (Ascorbyl palmitate)	A	V	V	M	
E306	Extracts of natural origin rich in tocopherols		V	V	M	Vitamin E
E307	Synthetic *alpha*-tocopherol				M	
E308	Synthetic *gamma*-tocopherol				M	
E309	Synthetic *delta*-tocopherol				M	
E310	Propyl gallate				M	
E311	Octyl gallate				M	
E312	Dodecyl gallate				M	
E320	Butylated hydroxyanisole (BHA)				M	
E321	Butylated hydroxytoluene (BHT)				M	

Emulsifiers, stabilizers, thickeners

		Animal	Vegetarian	Vegan	Mineral
E322	Lecithins	A	V	V	
E325	Sodium lactate	A	V		M
E326	Potassium lactate	A	V		M
E327	Calcium lactate	A	V	V	
E330	Citric acid		V	V	
E331	Sodium dihydrogen citrate (*mono*Sodium citrate), *di*Sodium citrate, *tri*Sodium citrate				M
E332	Potassium dihydrogen citrate (*mono*Potassium citrate), *tri*Potassium citrate				M

E333	*mono*Calcium citrate, *di*Calcium citrate, *tri*Calcium citrate	A			M
E334	L-(+)-tartaric acid	A	V		M
E335	*mono*Sodium (L-(+)-tartrate, *di*Sodium L-(+)-tartrate		V	V	M
E336	*mono*Potassium L-(+)-tartrate (Cream of tartar), *di*Potassium L-(+)-tartrate		V	V	M
E337	Potassium sodium L-(+)-tartrate		V	V	M
E338	Orthophosphoric acid (Phosphoric acid)	A			M
E339	Sodium dihydrogen orthophosphate, *di*Sodium hydrogen orthophosphate, *tri*Sodium orthophosphate	A			M
E340	Potassium dihydrogen orthophosphate, *di*Potassium hydrogen orthophosphate, *tri*Potassium orthophosphate	A			M
E341	Calcium tetrahydrogen diorthophosphate, Calcium hydrogen orthophosphate, *tri*Calcium diorthophosphate	A			M
350	Sodium malate, sodium hydrogen malate	A	V	V	M
351	Potassium malate		V	V	M
352	Calcium malate, calcium hydrogen malate		V	V	M
353	Metatartaric acid	A	V		M

	Animal	Vegetarian	Vegan	Mineral
355 Adipic acid		V	V	M
363 Succinzic acid		V	V	M
370 1,4-Heptonolactone				M
375 Nicotinic acid				M
380 triAmmonium citrate				M
381 Ammonium ferric citrate				M
385 Calcium disodium ethylenediamine – NNN'N'-tetra-acetate (Calcium disodium E D T A)				M
E400 Alginic acid		V	V	M
E401 Sodium alginate		V	V	M
E402 Potassium alginate		V	V	M
E403 Ammonium alginate		V	V	M
E404 Calcium alginate	A	V	V	
E405 Propane-1,2-diol alginate (Propylene glycol alginate)		V	V	M
E406 Agar		V	V	
E407 Carrageenan		V	V	
E410 Locust bean gum (Carob gum)		V	V	
E412 Guar gum		V	V	
E413 Tragacanth		V	V	
E414 Gum arabic (Acacia)		V	V	
E415 Xanthan gum		V	V	
416 Karaya gum		V	V	

Synthetic sweeteners

E420	Sorbitol, sorbitol syrup				M
E421	Mannitol				M
E422	Glycerol	A	rarely	rarely	M
430	Polyoxyethylene (8) stearate	A			M
431	Polyoxyethylene (40) stearate	A			M
432	Polyoxyethylene (20) sorbitan monolaurate (Polysorbate 20)	A			M
433	Polyoxyethylene (20) sorbitan mono-oleate (Polysorbate 80)	A			M
434	Polyoxyethylene (20) sorbitan monopalmitate (Polysorbate 40)	A			M
435	Polyoxyethylene (20) sorbitan monostearate (Polysorbate 60)	A			M
436	Polyoxyethylene (20) sorbitan tristearate (Polysorbate 65)	A			M

Emulsifiers, stabilizers, thickeners

E440(a)	Pectin		V	V	
E440(b)	Amidated pectin		V	V	
442	Ammonium phosphatides				M
E450(a)	diSodium dihydrogen diphosphate, triSodium diphosphate, tetraSodium diphosphate				M

	Animal	Vegetarian	Vegan	Mineral
diphosphate, *tetra*Potassium diphosphate	A			M
E450(b) *penta*Sodium triphosphate, *penta*Potassium triphosphate	A			M
E450(c) Sodium polyphosphates, Potassium polyphosphates	A			M
E460 Microcrystalline cellulose, alpha-cellulose (Powdered cellulose)		V	V	M
E461 Methylcellulose		V	V	M
E463 Hydroxypropylcellulose		V	V	M
E464 Hydroxypropylmethylcellulose		V	V	M
E465 Ethylmethylcellulose		V	V	M
E466 Carboxymethylcellulose, sodium salt (CMC)		V	V	M
E470 Sodium, potassium and calcium salts of fatty acids	A	V	V	M
E471 Mono- and di-glycerides of fatty acids	A	V	V	M
E472(a) Acetic acid esters of mono- and di-glycerides of fatty acids	A	V	V	M
E472(b) Lactic acid esters of mono- and di-glycerides of fatty acids (Lactoglycerides)	A	V	V	M

E472(c)	Citric acid esters of mono- and di-glycerides of fatty acids (Citroglycerides)	A	V		M
E472(e)	Mono- and diacetyltartaric acid esters of mono- and di-glycerides of fatty acids	A	V	V	M
E473	Sucrose esters of fatty acids	A	V	V	M
E474	Sucroglycerides	A	V	V	M
E475	Polyglycerol esters of fatty acids	A	V	V	M
476	Polyglycerol esters of polycondensed fatty acids of castor oil (Polyglycerol polyricinoleate)		V	V	M
E477	Propane-1,2-diol esters of fatty acids	A	V	V	M
478	Lactylated fatty acid esters of glycerol and propane-1,2-diol	A	V	V	M
E481	Sodium stearoyl-2-lactylate	A	V	V	M
E482	Calcium stearoyl-2-lactylate	A	V	V	M
E483	Stearyl tartrate	A	V	V	M
491	Sorbitan monostearate	A	V	V	M
492	Sorbitan tristearate	A	V	V	M
493	Sorbitan monolaurate				M
494	Sorbitan mono-oleate				M
495	Sorbitan monopalmitate				M
500	Sodium carbonate, Sodium hydrogen carbonate (Bicarbonate of soda), Sodium sesquicarbonate		V	V	M

Acids, bases

		Animal	Vegetarian	Vegan	Mineral
501	Potassium carbonate, Potassium hydrogen carbonate				M
503	Ammonium carbonate, Ammonium hydrogen carbonate				
504	Magnesium carbonate				M
507	Hydrochloric acid				M
508	Potassium chloride				M
509	Calcium chloride				M
510	Ammonium chloride				M
513	Sulphuric acid				M
514	Sodium sulphate				M
515	Potassium sulphate				M
516	Calcium sulphate				M
518	Magnesium sulphate				M
524	Sodium hydroxide				M
525	Potassium hydroxide				M
526	Calcium hydroxide				M
527	Ammonium hydroxide				M
528	Magnesium hydroxide				M
529	Calcium oxide				M

Anti-caking agents

		Animal	Vegetarian	Vegan	Mineral
530	Magnesium oxide				M
535	Sodium ferrocyanide (Sodium hexacyanoferrate II)				M

536	Potassium ferrocyanide (Potassium hexacyanoferrate II)			M
540	*di*Calcium diphosphate			M
541	Sodium aluminium phosphate			M
542	Edible bone phosphate	A		
544	Calcium polyphosphates			M
545	Ammonium polyphosphates			M
551	Silicon dioxide (Silica)			M
552	Calcium silicate			M
553(a)	Magnesium silicate synthetic, Magnesium trisilicate			M
553(b)	Talc			M
554	Aluminium sodium silicate			M
556	Aluminium calcium silicate			M
558	Bentonite			
559	Kaolin			
570	Stearic acid	A	V	
572	Magnesium stearate	A	V	M
575	D-glucono-1,5-lactone (Glucono *delta*-lactone)			M
576	Sodium gluconate			M
577	Potassium gluconate			M
578	Calcium gluconate		M	

Flavour enhancers, sweeteners

620	L-glutamic acid			M
621	Sodium hydrogen L-glutamate (*mono*Sodium glutamate or MSG)	V	V	M

		Animal	Vegetarian	Vegan	Mineral
622	Potassium hydrogen L-glutamate (*mono*Potassium glutamate)				M
623	Calcium dihydrogen di-L-glutamate (Calcium glutamate)				M
627	Guanosine 5'-(disodium phosphate) (Sodium guanylate)	A			
631	Inosine 5'-(disodium phosphate) (Sodium inosinate)	A	V	∨	
635	Sodium 5'-ribonucleotide				M
636	Maltol				M
637	Ethyl maltol				M

Glazing agents

		Animal	Vegetarian	Vegan	Mineral
900	Dimethylpolysiloxane				M
901	Beeswax	A			
903	Carnauba wax		V	∨	
904	Shellac	A			
905	Mineral hydrocarbons				M
907	Refined microcrystalline wax				M

Improving and bleaching agents

920	L-cysteine hydrochloride	A	M
924	Potassium bromate		M
925	Chlorine		M
926	Chlorine dioxide		M
927	Azodicarbonamide		M
	(Azoformamide)		

No E numbers

Sweeteners

–	Saccharin			M
–	Saccharin calcium			M
–	Saccharin sodium			M
–	Aspartame	A		M
–	Acesulfame potassium			M
–	Thaumatin*		V	V
–	Hydrogenated glucose syrup		V	V
–	Isomalt			M
–	Xylitol		V	V

* Vegetable source of amino acids mixture of proteins from W. African fruit occurs widely in natural fruit and vegetables

Solvents

–	Ethyl alcohol		V	V
–	Ethyl acetate		V	V
–	Diethyl ether		V	V

	Animal	Vegetarian	Vegan	Mineral
— Glycerol monoacetate		V	V	M
— Glycerol triacetate		V	V	M
— Isopropyl alcohol		V	V	M
— Propylene glycol				M

Miscellaneous

	Animal	Vegetarian	Vegan	Mineral
— Ethoxyquin				M
— Dioctyl sodium sulphosuccinate				M
— Extract of quillaia		V	V	M
— Dichlorodifluoromethane				M
— Calcium phytate		V	V	M
— Glycine	A	V	V	M
— Sodium heptonate				M*
— Calcium heptonate				M*
— Hydrogen				M
— Nitrogen				M
— Nitrous oxide				M
— Oxygen				M
— Octadeyl ammonium acetate				M
— Oxystearin	A			

* Or biologically derived.

Source: Janette Marshall, *Shopping for Health*, Penguin, 1987.

THE VEGETARIAN LARDER

If you don't eat meat or fish you will need to find other sources of protein and the vegetarian larder offers wide scope for imaginative meals using beans, peas, lentils, grains and nuts and seeds.

For the vegetarian in a hurry there is more interest in the quicker-cooking varieties and in convenience foods which can stock the shelves. But if you are habitually busy you may risk missing out on some nutrients, so the suggestions for stocking the larder have been made with healthy-eating criteria in mind.

If you already have a 'wholefood' larder, you might be interested in some new items listed in this section. If healthy eating is a new priority, you will find simple explanations about why some foods are chosen in preference to others.

BARLEY

Barley is a whole grain that can combine with legumes or nuts and seeds to give vegetarian protein. It is most commonly seen as pearl barley which is a refined grain that has had its bran and some of the germ milled off. The unrefined barley is called pot barley or scotch barley, but this is not a quick grain to use. It takes at least an hour to boil, but it can be used as a change from rice, or as a grain in casseroles and soups.

BEANS

Dried beans and pulses are an important source of protein in the vegetarian diet, but for the cook in a hurry most of them take too long to soak and boil. However, the longer-cooking ones can be cooked in batches and then frozen for later use, or you could use the more convenient canned ready-cooked beans and pulses listed in this section. Personally, I don't think there is much point in boiling a large quantity of beans and then using them in different dishes each day because eating too much of the same food, even in different 'disguises', is boring and defeats the object of a healthy mixed diet.

Faster-cooking beans

There are a few beans that you can use from scratch and still have a meal on the table quickly.

Adzuki beans

These are small, dark red beans. After an overnight soak, or a couple of hours in boiling water in a vacuum food flask, they can be boiled in forty to forty-five minutes or pressure-cooked in fifteen minutes at high pressure.

Mung beans

These are small, dark green beans, more often used in their sprouted form as beansprouts in Chinese dishes. After an overnight soak, or a couple of hours in boiling water in a food flask, they can be boiled for thirty minutes or pressure-cooked in fifteen minutes at high pressure.

Black-eye beans

These are quite small, creamy-coloured beans with a black 'eye', often called cowpeas in American cookery books. They do not have to be soaked overnight but will cook quicker if they have been soaked or left in boiling water in a food flask for a couple of hours. They will cook in thirty minutes and ten – fifteen minutes in a pressure-cooker.

PULSES

Lentils

Brown (or Puy) lentils are whole lentils and smaller than the green and flattish continental lentils, which are also whole. Split red lentils have had their outer casing removed and are very quick to cook. They easily disintegrate into a purée. Brown and continental lentils will cook in twenty-five to thirty minutes. Split red lentils cook in fifteen minutes. Lentils do not need pre-soaking and they are not really suitable for use in a pressure-cooker.

Peas

Split peas are yellow or green in colour and are the dried version of the peas which we more commonly eat fresh. They do not need pre-soaking, but cooking will be quicker if they are soaked. They will boil in about thirty to forty minutes and can be pressure-cooked in fifteen minutes on high pressure. Whole green peas take much longer to cook (sixty minutes) and do need pre-soaking.

Canned beans

These have already been cooked so you can use them straight from the can either in cold dishes such as salads or to make into dips and pâtés or in hot dishes. Add them towards the end of cooking or they will disintegrate.

Canned beans invariably have salt and/or sugar added. Unfortunately this is one of the disadvantages to be set against the convenience they offer. Some varieties also contain additives such as calcium chloride which is a sequestrant. Sequestrants bind with traces of metal present in canned food which otherwise would contaminate it or cause oxidation to make some foods rancid or 'off'.

Most supermarkets have their own and other brands of canned red kidney beans and butter beans. Some supermarkets have also chickpeas, borlotti beans, brown beans, pinto beans and white kidney beans. They are usually canned in water but contain sugar, salt and sequestrants.

Baked beans

Usually the haricot (or navy) bean from the United States, canned in tomato sauce made from tomatoes, modified starch, vinegar and spices, with added salt and sugar. There are some no-added-sugar varieties including Whole Earth Campfire-Style baked beans and Waitrose no-added-sugar. Keep your eyes open for new brands. Heinz Weight-Watchers, Crosse & Blackwell Healthy Balance and Sainsbury's offer reduced amounts of added salt and sugar and HP have reduced by half the sugar in their beans. Heinz Weight-Watchers beans are free from sugar but they contain the artificial sweetener, saccharin.

BISCUITS

As you know, biscuits are (or should be!) for treats only because they can add considerable fat and sugar to the diet, leaving less room for more nutritious foods. Most manufacturers use cheap hydrogenated fats (see p. 7) and few biscuits are made from wholemeal flour.

The main area of concern for vegetarians and vegans is avoiding animal fats and generally this means buying biscuits from a health-food shop. However, larger manufacturers, recognizing the profits to be made from the health market, are changing their recipes. Here is a selection of the better buys, which are all free from artificial additives. Vegans should check individual varieties for eggs and honey.

Allinsons biscuits are made with wholemeal flour, unrefined sugar and vegetable fats. There are thirteen varieties including carob-coated biscuits (see carob p. 43).

Country Basket biscuits are made with wheatmeal flour, raw cane sugar and vegetable fats.

Holly Mill biscuits are made with wholemeal flour, brown sugar and vegetable fats. Some varieties contain eggs.

Braycott biscuits are based on wholemeal flour and/or oats, plus vegetable fats and raw sugar and/or molasses. Some are carob-coated.

Digestive biscuits are made by many biscuit manufacturers and most contain animal fats. Health-food-shop brands that don't are Mitchelhill digestives (but they do contain honey) and Doves Farm, made with organic flour. Doves Farm also sell digestives coated with carob in the style of chocolate biscuits, carob bourbons and ginger-nuts.

Some large manufacturers have ranges which include a number of products suitable for vegetarians.

Fox's biscuits produce some additive-free biscuits made with wholemeal flour. These include Bran Crunch, Wholemeal Honey Sandwich and Muesli biscuits which are suitable for vegetarians. Bran Crunch is a possible for vegans; the others contain honey. There are other vegetarian biscuits from Fox's, but they are not wholefood.

McVities (part of United Biscuits) has a range called Natural Choice which is free from additives and made with wholemeal flour/oats and vegetable fats. Two varieties contain yoghurt, but the others are also suitable for vegans.

BREAD

The basic choice here is between wholemeal and brown or white bread. Wholemeal has the advantage of containing the goodness of the whole grain, which includes fibre, vitamins and minerals. Brown may be white flour, coloured with caramel. White will have had the bran and wheatgerm removed, along with the vitamins and minerals destroyed by the powerful bleaching agents used to whiten the flour. However, white bread is fortified by law and has calcium, iron, and vitamins B_1 (thiamin) and B_3 (niacin) added. Many additives are allowed in the modern factory steam-baking of bread. Most are allowed in white breads, but wholemeal contains fewer improvers, although it may contain preservatives and emulsifiers. You will have to read the label of wrapped breads in order to avoid additives or look out for signs in bakers' shops which should be displayed near the bread if it contains additives. Alternatively ask your baker if additives are used and what the flour he uses contains.

There are some special breads free from additives and suitable for vegetarians and vegans – unless otherwise stated.

Vogel is made from wheat flour with added grains, wheat protein, bran and rye flour and grains. But it is not suitable for vegans because it contains whey powder. It is widely available.

Whole Earth bread is a wholemeal loaf with added grains and seeds, plus soya flour, carrots and kelp. It can be obtained from health-food shops.

Boots the Chemist sell a range of wholemeal breads (and cakes) made from Prewett's stoneground flour. These do include the 'safe' improver E300 and L- ascorbic acid – a type of vitamin C.

Doves Farm loaf is made from organic wholemeal flour.

Spring Hill bread is made from wholemeal, wheat and rye flours, with added sprouted grains. They are dense loaves of a pumpernickel or rye-bread texture.

Hovis is not a wholemeal loaf, but it has a lot of added wheatgerm. This gives it a soft texture and its characteristic flavour but does not contain vitamin E as this is destroyed during baking. It contains an emulsifier of vegetable origin.

VitBe wheatgerm bread is virtually identical to Hovis.

Allinsons loaves are made from ordinary or from stoneground wholemeal flour. They contain an emulsifier of vegetable origin and sugar but have a reduced level of salt.

Soreen Wholemeal Fruitmalt loaf has raisins and is additive free. It does contain whey and whey protein and so is not suitable for vegans.

Breadcrumbs

It's now possible to buy packets of dried breadcrumbs that are wholemeal and free from artificial colours such as tartrazine which make them bright orange. Brands include Mr Harvey's Original Wholemeal, Just Naturally and Supercook.

BREAKFAST CEREALS

You are looking for wholegrain breakfast cereals that do not have much, if any, added salt and sugar. Added bran shouldn't be necessary, either, if the whole of the grain is included in the cereal. There are a few cereals free from added salt and sugar. They are:
- Nabisco's Shredded Wheat and Cubs
- Quaker's Puffed Wheat
- Sainsbury's Miniwheats and Puffed Wheat
- Kellogg's Nutritime range

Muesli

You can buy no-added-sugar varieties or you can make your own at home. Make in batches and store in an airtight container. Mix together rolled oats, millet flakes, rye flakes, dried fruit, nuts and seeds. Add fresh fruit just before serving.

No-added-sugar mueslis:

- Cheshire Wholefoods
- Just Naturally
- Familia Swiss Birchermuesli
- Waitrose
- Sainsbury's
- Boots Second Nature
- Tesco
- Kellogg's Summer Orchard
- Sunwheel
- Jordans Special Recipe
- Doves Farm
- Bejam

Porridge

This is one of the most natural and nutritious breakfast cereals. It can be made using rolled oats or oatmeal which comes as fine, medium or coarse. For quick cooking choose rolled oats or fine oatmeal. You can make as 'creamy' porridge cooking the oats with water or with skimmed milk (see pp. 6 and 14 for soluble fibre benefits).

Granola

It is a crunchy breakfast cereal usually based on oats and dried fruits which are baked with sugar, honey or syrup. There are now three varieties free from added sugar and salt: Whole Earth Orange Crunch and Almond Crunch and Jordans Original Crunchy Natural.

BUCKWHEAT

Buckwheat is a small, dark triangular grain that can combine with legumes or nuts and seeds to give vegetarian protein. It is widely grown and used in Eastern Europe and is valuable for the vegetarian or vegan in a hurry because it cooks quickly – about fifteen minutes' boiling time. It can be used in place of rice or other grains and has a slightly sweet, nutty flavour.

Buckwheat is also milled into a wholegrain flour which is a grey-brown colour and sold in health-food shops. It makes delicious thin crêpes or pancakes for sweet or savoury dishes.

BULGUR

This is another name for the cracked wheat grain which can also be combined with legumes or nuts and seeds to provide vegetarian protein. Because the wheat has been soaked, then parched in the sun and cracked or lightly milled, it is partially cooked and so takes only fifteen to twenty minutes to cook. It is very handy for salads but can be eaten, like rice, with other foods or used in soups and casseroles.

BURGERS

Burgers are one of the most popular meat-based convenience and fast foods, but vegetarian burgers are equally quick and much more appealing to the healthy eater because they are usually low in fat and high in fibre. You can buy them fresh or frozen or as a store-cupboard standby in the form of dry packet mixes. Vegetarians can mix and bind them with water, milk or eggs and vegans can use water or soya milk. All are suitable for vegetarians and vegans and are free from additives – unless otherwise stated.

Packet burger mixes

These usually claim more protein and less fat than meat burgers. All are free from additives and suitable for vegetarians and vegans – unless otherwise stated.

Vege Burger range is Herb and Vegetable, Chilli and No Salt. Mix with egg and/or water. The pack makes four burgers.

Boots Vegetable Burger Mix is mixed with water. The pack makes eight burgers.

Hera range is Spicy, Savoury, Barbecue and Shawburger (named after George Bernard Shaw, it contains cheese and so is not for vegans). Mix with water. The pack makes four burgers.

CANNED FRUIT AND VEGETABLES

Your store-cupboard or larder will probably have room for some canned vegetables, if not for fruit as well. Although these are best fresh, there are some occasions when you will be glad of canned produce. While fresh fruit and vegetables lose vitamins and minerals during the time it takes from their harvesting to the shop shelf and then to being bought, canned goods could often be fresher than they are. For example, Green Giant sweetcorn canners claim the time from harvesting to canning can be as little as forty-five minutes. Canned vegetables extend the range of vegetarian and vegan dishes you can make by, for example, supplying water chestnuts and bamboo shoots for Chinese food, and ackee and other exotic fruits for Caribbean food.

An increasing variety of canned produce without added salt or syrup and additives is becoming available. This will be stated on the label, but beware of cans proclaiming 'No Preservatives' or 'No Colourings'. It's worth reading the ingredients listing because the can may often contain other additives you might wish to avoid.

Fruit canned in juice is available from John West, Red Sail, Del Monte, Valfrutta, Pickerings, Chivers, Lockwoods and the supermarket own brands.

Fruit canned in water from Dietade is found in health-food shops. Red Sail offer apple slices.

Vegetables without sugar and salt are available from Del Monte, and sweetcorn from Green Giant.

Canned tomatoes are available in many brands and are invariably in natural tomato juice, usually with added salt. They are also available in cartons from Cirio and Napolina.

CAROB AND CHOCOLATE

These are not an essential part of any vegetarian or vegan's storecupboard, but if you like home-baking you will probably find them, at some time, on your shopping list.

Carob is the 'healthy' alternative to chocolate. It comes in bars or in powder form like cocoa and is made from the roasted and ground Mediterranean carob pod, free from caffeine, theobromine and oxalic acid. The first two are stimulants and may trigger migraines. Oxalic acid blocks the absorption of calcium and zinc needed for a complexion free from spots.

Carob is naturally sweeter than cocoa, so in some products no sugar is added. Carob also tends to be lower in fat and the fats are often vegetable (usually soya) rather than dairy fats. However vegans should still be wary of the skimmed milk used in some bars.

Kalibu carob bars in several flavours are available either as standard (using raw cane sugar) or in no added-sugar varieties. These are suitable for vegetarians but not for vegans as they contain skimmed milk powder.

Plamil soya-based carob bar is entirely animal-free and called non-dairy carob. Plamil also make a plain chocolate with soya bar which is a non-dairy chocolate for vegans.

COFFEE

You may prefer a decaffeinated coffee to avoid the side-effects of caffeine which stimulates gastric juices, acts as a diuretic, may keep you awake at night, may raise blood-fat levels (especially cholesterol) and blood-sugar levels, and may cause women to have lumpy or painful breasts. Pregnant women are advised to cut down on caffeine.

The decaffeination methods – chemical solvent, carbon dioxide method, water-processing – do not involve animal products. De-caffeinated coffee comes as soluble instant coffee, ready-ground vacuum-packed coffee and as coffee beans. It can be obtained from tea and coffee merchants, supermarkets, food halls, health-food and wholefood shops.

COUSCOUS

There are several methods given for making this partially cooked grain which can be combined with legumes or nuts and seeds to make vegetarian protein. Couscous may be made with rolled semolina to form tiny grains or it may be made with bulgur (cracked wheat). Either way, it is very quick to cook and can be used where you would use any other grain, although traditionally it was cooked in steam over a meat stew or casserole.

CRISPS

Crisps are high in fat and salt and are a very expensive way of eating potatoes. In Britain more than five thousand million packets a year are eaten. Because crisps are so high in fat, preservatives are used to lengthen their shelf life and the commonly used BHA and BHT antioxidants are not accepted by everyone as 'safe'.

Vegetarians and vegans may want to limit their intake so more valuable foods are not pushed out of their diet. Apart from avoiding the obvious animal-related crisp flavours, or cheese ones for vegans, the varieties lower in fat and salt may be chosen. These are only additive-free if stated.

Low fat and salt crisps

Smiths Salt 'n Shake are unsalted, unless you add the salt in the little blue bag.

Smiths Square Crisps claim to contain 25 per cent less fat than standard crisps.

KP Lower Fat Crisps claim to have 30 per cent less fat than standard crisps, and have a lightly salted variety, *but* these crisps contain lactose (milk sugar) and so are unsuitable for vegans.

St Michael Lower Fat, Lightly Salted claim to have 30 per cent less fat than standard crisps.

Sooner Foods plain and salted crisps are free from additives.

A *Which?* report in August 1986 analysed some of the crisps claiming to have less fat than standard kinds and found St Michael to be lowest with 22g per 100g (compared with standard 38–9g). KP were next with 23g and Smiths Square had 28g.

Alternative 'crisps'

There are some alternatives to crisps which are made with wholemeal flour rather than potatoes and are available from health-food shops. The wholemeal dough is deep-fried and the 'crisps' are flavoured or salted. All are suitable for vegetarians and vegans – unless otherwise stated.

Wholewheat Crisps are ready salted and fried in groundnut oil.

Wheat Eats are baked rather than fried, so they are lower in fat and calories. All, except cheese, are suitable for vegans.

Crispy Soybits are made with soya protein and rice and are flavoured with spices and herbs. They are also low in fat.

Tortilla Chips and Corn Chips are made from maize or corn and fried in vegetable oil. The first ones were made by Phileas Fogg, but other brands include Marks & Spencer and Meximan which is sold in health-food shops.

CRISPBREAD

Crispbreads are handy store-cupboard foods because they are high in fibre, low in fat and keep well without the use of preservatives. Unlike biscuits, they are usually free from animal fats, although some do contain added skimmed milk powder which vegans will wish to avoid. All are additive-free – unless otherwise stated.

Ryvita is a wholemeal rye flour range with all, except Crackerbread (skimmed milk), suitable for vegetarians and vegans.

Ryking wholemeal wheat and rye flour crispbreads are suitable for vegetarians and vegans with the exception of Crispbread Snack (cheese) and Golden Wheat (whey, skimmed milk).

Kalvi wholemeal rye flour range are all suitable for vegetarians and vegans.

Primula wholemeal rye flour crispbreads are all suitable for vegetarians and vegans.

Energen range is based on wholemeal, brown or rye flours but none are suitable for vegans as they contain skimmed milk, cheese or whey.

Ideal wholegrain crispbreads are all suitable for vegetarians and vegans.

Scandacrisp wholemeal rye flour crispbreads are suitable for vegetarians and vegans.

<u>GG Bran</u> crispbreads with added bran are suitable for vegetarians and vegans and can be bought from health-food shops.

<u>Rice Crispbread</u> is primarily for those intolerant to wheat or gluten, but tasty for vegetarians and vegans. It uses soya milk powder instead of skimmed milk powder.

CUSTARD

Real custard is made with eggs, milk and sugar – the eggs thicken and colour the mixture. Most custard powders use cheap, refined starch thickeners, fats, sugar and colourings. But there are now some that might be acceptable to vegetarians and to those vegans who might make soya milk custard.

<u>Mr Merry</u> Instant Custard Mix is from health-food shops and is sold in sachets that make up 1pt/600ml to produce a pouring custard that sets if left. It contains raw cane sugar, guar gum, carageenan, lecithin, natural vanilla and annatto to colour the mixture.

<u>Boots Custard Powder</u> also uses natural colouring and is free from other additives.

<u>Golden Archer</u> and <u>Granny Ann</u> canned custards are additive-free and made from soya milk. They are available from health-food shops.

ESSENCES

Many recipes call for flavourings such as vanilla, almond, orange, lemon, peppermint, etc., and these are sold in the form of artificial flavours in some shops. However real extracts, or essences derived from the actual nuts, fruits or plants, are available and are preferable to the chemically made versions. You will find them in health-food shops or specialist shops, such as Culpeper's herbalists.

FLOUR

Here you are faced with the same choice as with bread – white or wholemeal? Switching to, or using, wholemeal adds fibre, vitamins and minerals. It also adds flavour! There are two main extraction rates of wholemeal flour: 100 per cent – which contains all the grain – and 81 per cent which has had some bran and wheatgerm sieved out. Modern roller-milling is fast and hot so some of the heat-sensitive B vitamins are lost. That's why traditional slow-milling, using stone millstones, is sometimes preferred because more of the B vitamins and vitamin E survive. Brown flour may have an 85–90 per cent extraction rate, or it may be less because it can simply be white flour that has been coloured with caramel. There is also an 85 per cent wholemeal flour. These may seem odd percentages but they were developed after the Second World War when, by law, millers had to enrich white flour by putting back vitamins, calcium and iron to the amount found in 80 per cent extraction-rate flour. So 81 per cent brown flour was introduced for people who wanted a 'white' flour that was unbleached and had nothing added to it.

You might also like to have Granary flour in your store-cupboard. This is a brown flour to which malted grains have been added. Granary is a trade name and similar flours go by the name of malted flours. They are not wholemeal. There are many brands of wholemeal flours and you may want to choose a nationally available brand or a local brand. Some of the bigger names to ask for are Allinsons, Prewett's and Jordans. Other good, but smaller brands, are Doves Farm, Marriages, Pimhill and St Nicholas.

FRUIT

Dried fruit

It is often treated with preservatives such as sulphur dioxide (E220) and potassium sorbate (E202). This is only for cosmetic purposes since drying the fruit actually preserves it – the sulphites keep its colour. Sulphites are some of the most troublesome and widespread additives in British food. Mineral oils such as liquid paraffin are used to coat some dried fruit. This is another cosmetic practice of no nutritional value and it may even be a problematic one because, like sulphites, these oils can have an adverse effect on vitamins in the fruit and in the body. Glacé cherries and some candied peels will also contain artificial colouring.

Unsulphured fruit and dried fruit without mineral oil can be obtained from health-food shops, but you are unlikely to find unsorbated prunes or unsulphured exotic light fruits because they are dark and less attractive if untreated. However, Hunza apricots, a form of small wild apricot, are untreated, as are dates and figs. Sometimes health-food shops use vegetable oils to give the fruit a glossy sheen. Some 'sun-dried' varieties on sale in other shops are also free from additives. Several brands of glacé cherries produced with a natural colour, anthocyanin (from grape skins), are available from health-food shops and supermarkets.

Ready-to-eat and no-need-to-soak varieties of dried fruit have been partially rehydrated so they are softer and less concentrated. It takes about 6lb (2.7kg) fresh peaches to make 1lb (450g) of the dried fruit but only half that amount to make 1lb (450g) of this 'convenience' fruit.

GRAVY

Something that vegetarians and vegans may enjoy with a nutroast but which differs from the sauce made of meat juices. You can base gravy on a vegetable bouillon or stock cube (pp. 61–2) and then use something like Pantry Stock Gravy Mix or Applefords Low Salt Gravymix made with wholemeal flour, herbs and spices and available from health-food shops.

HERBS

Both fresh and dried herbs are an invaluable part of vegetarian and vegan (or any other) cooking. Fresh herbs are especially useful for quick cooking. Their flavour is spoilt by long cooking and they are best stirred in either at the end, or towards the end, of cooking.

Fresh herbs are now available from supermarkets. The most readily available are parsley, mint, sage, bay leaves, coriander, chives, chervil, thyme, basil and ready-mixed bouquet garnis of parsley, bay leaves and thyme. A tablespoonful of freshly chopped herbs will enliven many dishes. You can also keep a selection of dried herbs for the winter. Buy in small amounts and store in a cool, dark place or dry your own in double-quick time in the microwave.

HONEY

Honey is an alternative to sugar. Although it has much folklore attached to it and many claims for its 'health-giving' properties, it remains a sugar and should be treated as such (see discussion on sugar and diet p. 13). However it is made up of glucose and fructose (p. 62) and is therefore less disruptive to blood-sugar levels than table sugar. It can be used for cooking but remember it is 20 per cent water, so it will change the consistency of your recipes. Honey is sold either clear or set. For most kitchen use, clear is better because it's easier to work with. If buying for cooking, choose a mild-flavoured and light-coloured honey that is not overpowering – unless you want the dish to taste only of honey! Some vegans may not want to use honey because it is the product of insects.

JAM

No problems here with animal products, but there are some 'healthier' jams with reduced sugar or even without any added sugar.

No-added-sugar jams

These jams and marmalades are available in health-food shops and some supermarkets. Brands to look out for are: Whole Earth, Country Basket, Nature's Store, Ethos and Safeway's own brand.

Reduced sugar jams

These are made by Robertson's, who call their range Today's Recipe, and by Energen, De L'Ora and Streamline. They all contain additives.

The alternative to conventional jams which often contain additives is Extra Jam – a category with more fruit than standard jams and jellies and not allowed to contain additives.

Health-food shops also stock Thursday Cottage and Delicia brands of preserves made with raw cane sugar and free from additives.

MARZIPAN

The traditional recipe for marzipan contains sugar, almonds and eggs but modern marzipans add colouring to give the yellow shade and leave out the eggs. Hence, vegans can use this marzipan. There are also some marzipans free from artificial colouring. These include Whitworths white marzipan and some supermarkets do their own label white marzipan. Health-food shops stock marzipan made with raw cane sugar. Two brands are Prewett's and Ethos.

MAIZE

Maize does not have as good a balance of amino-acids (p. 4) as other grains and so is not as valuable for combining with legumes or nuts and seeds to make vegetable protein. It is more commonly used as popcorn (p. 57) and as maize flour which makes the classic Italian dish, polenta. It is also popular in South American and Caribbean corn bread and muffins – neither of which is a quick convenience food although corn bread can be frozen and then thawed quite quickly.

MALT

Jars of malt can often be seen in health-food shops as it is an alternative sweetener for baking. It is a by-product of malting barley used for brewing and free from animal products and additives. It can be used in many recipes and is less sweet than sugar, but should still be treated as a sugar (see p. 13 for discussion on sugar). Two brands to look out for are Cookie Malt and Barley Malt Syrup from Sunwheel.

MINCEMEAT

This is traditionally made with suet and is high in sugar, but now there are brands which vegetarians and vegans can enjoy. These are all from health-food shops and all are additive-free.

Prewett's is made with raw cane sugar and vegetable fat.

Down to Earth is free from sugar and fat and after opening has to be kept in the fridge. It also includes some organic fruit.

De L'Ora Exotic is free from sugar, but it does contain honey and vegetable fat.

NUTS

Meat-eaters might erroneously think that vegetarians live on nut cutlets and while there are many other foods available to non-meat-eaters, nuts do play quite a large part in the diet. They are, however, high in calories because of their natural oils and so, like cheese, should be used in moderation. Some nuts are also higher in saturated fats than others (see Table 2 opposite).

Nuts can be bought in many forms – in their shells or shelled, whole or split as pieces, flaked or ground. They are a good source of B vitamins, lecithin and minerals. Vitamin E is also found in the natural oils of many nuts. The minerals most commonly associated with nuts are magnesium and potassium. Nuts also contain fibre, especially almonds and coconuts. The only nut to contain vitamin C is the coconut which has a small amount in its flesh and in the liquid inside.

Snack foods

Nuts are also snack foods and here they are particularly popular roasted and salted. In most cases this adds fats and calories to an already high-calorie food. Invariably, it also means the addition of antioxidants as preservatives to prevent rancidity. However, there are some brands available which do not have these disadvantages.

Marks & Spencer peanuts are roasted without added fat and salt.

Sooner Foods peanuts are roasted and salted, but free from additives.

KP Roasted Salted peanuts are free from additives.

Macadamia nuts are sometimes roasted without additional fat but often coconut oil is used – adding to the total of saturated fat in an already highly saturated and fatty nut. Sea salt is usually added but macadamias are free from additives.

OATS

Oats may be cooked like brown rice or any other grain in boiling water, and used as a grain or eaten with legumes or nuts and seeds to provide complete vegetarian protein. But oats take a long time to cook and rolled oats is much quicker for the cook in a hurry. Oats

TABLE 2

Nutritional Contents of Nuts

Grams per 4oz (100g) shelled nut	Calories	Fat	Breakdown of Fat Content			Protein (g/100g)	Fibre
			Saturates	Mono-unsaturates	Poly-unsaturates		
Almond	565	53.5	8.3	71.6	19.6	16.9	14.3
Brazil	619	61.5	26.7	34.3	39.0	12.0	9.0
Cashew*	561	45.7	17.5	70.0	6.5	17.2	1.4
Chestnut	170	2.7	18.2	39.2	41.9	2.0	6.8
Coconut, fresh	351	36.0	83.0	7.0	1.8	3.2	13.6
Hazelnut	380	36.0	7.2	81.7	10.9	7.6	6.1
Peanut	570	49.0	15.2	50.1	29.8	24.3	8.1
Pecan*	687	71.2	7.0	63.2	19.6	9.2	2.3
Pistachio*	594	53.7	9.3	65.1	18.6	19.3	1.9
Walnut	525	51.5	11.4	16.3	71.4	10.6	5.2

Source: McCance and Widdowson, The Composition of Food, HMSO, 1985 (third impression). The nuts marked * are taken from the Handbook of Nutritional Contents of Foods, United States Department of Agriculture, 1975.

can be combined in pastry and crumble toppings, nut roasts and burgers, in baked foods such as flapjacks, and used to coat other foods such as burgers, rissoles and cutlets.

OILS

Vegetarians and vegans will probably make greater use of vegetable oils because choice of other fats is restricted by animal ingredients. Oils are liquid fats so the same health criteria apply with advice to cut down on saturated oils (for discussion on fats, see p. 7).

There are several types of processing available, ranging from cold-pressing to the use of chemical solvents to produce oils. Cold-pressing mechanically squeezes the oil from its source and doesn't use heat or chemicals, so little of the oil's natural content of vitamins and minerals is destroyed. The words 'cold-pressed' or 'unrefined' will be on the labels of these oils, which may have a sediment and are often darker in colour than the blended oils. These will have been processed, degummed, neutralized, washed, bleached and deodorized. There are several brands of unrefined oils to look out for in health-food shops, including Sunwheel, Western Isles, Harmony, Prewett's. Oils that are high in polyunsaturates include sunflower, safflower and soya but check that the source of the oil is named because a blended vegetable oil could contain saturated oils.

If you cook with oil do not be tempted to reuse it. Discard any oil that has darkened or froths.

PASTA

Pasta can be the basis of quick and convenient vegetarian meals. Far from being fattening, it is a starchy food that gives a steady release of energy and if you choose wholemeal pasta it will also be high in fibre. Most health-food shops and major multiples have their own brands of wholemeal pasta.

Dried pasta

Some brand names to look out for are:

Record Pasta is a complete range of dried wholemeal pasta in all shapes and sizes. For quicker dishes their Fasta Pasta offers partially cooked wholemeal and *verde* lasagne sheets which don't need boiling before you assemble the dish.

Euvita is an organic wholemeal pasta made in Holland from Italian durum wheat. They do a complete range of dried pastas.

Buitoni has a Country Harvest range made from white flour with added semolina and bran to give it the same amount of fibre as wholemeal.

Fresh pasta

This is available from supermarkets, delicatessens, etc. in either wholemeal, white or *verde* (made with spinach). Tagliatelle is the most useful for vegans, because the cannelloni, ravioli and tortellini are usually filled with meat or cheese. Vegetarians will find the ricotta-filled tortellini useful. Some also have tomato and mushroom sauce in sachets with the pasta. Names to ask for are Pasta Reale and Spaghetti House.

Canned pasta

This is usually spaghetti in tomato sauce but wholemeal canned pasta in a tomato sauce suitable for both vegetarians and vegans is now available from Crosse & Blackwell.

Pesto is a traditional Mediterranean sauce used to dress pasta. Based on herbs, pine kernels and Parmesan cheese, it's fine for vegetarians but not for vegans. Several brands are available and most don't have additives. Read the labels to check.

Noodles, ramen (Japanese noodles) and buckwheat pasta are also available from health-food shops. These cook as quickly as pasta and are also high in fibre.

PÂTÉ

Something traditionally for meat-eaters but vegetable pâtés are now available in health-food shops and some delicatessens. They may also be high in fat and calories but are lower in saturated fat than meat-based pâté. The names to ask for are:

<u>Cauldron Foods</u> vegetable or mushroom pâté

<u>Tartex</u> plain or herb pâté in tubes or tubs

<u>Leisure Vegetarian Golden Harvest</u>, mushroom and tropical pâtés

<u>Spring Hill Vegetarian</u> pâté produced from cold-pressed oils, herbs, vegetables and yeast

<u>Euvita Olive</u> pâté from organically produced olives, cold-pressed olive oil and herbs

<u>Better Fare</u> mushroom and hazelnut, tandoori lentil, brandy and lentil, cannellini bean pâtés

<u>La Source de Vie</u> organic sun pâté

<u>Vessen</u> pâté snacks – individual packs of pâté and bran oatcakes

<u>Granose</u> hazelnut pâté

<u>Sainsbury's</u> vegetable pâté, either pre-packed or from the delicatessen.

PEANUT BUTTER

A useful high-protein food for vegetarians and vegans, but it is also high in fat from the oils in the nuts and any oil added during manufacture. Health-food-shop peanut butters don't usually contain additives but a common additive used in others is E471 – an emulsifier which may be of animal or vegetable origin. If your favourite variety contains this, check with the makers about its origin. Other points to check for are added sugar and/or salt and added hydrogenated oils. The ingredients list will give you this information. Most widely available brands without additives are Boots Second Nature, Granose, Prewett's, Safeway, Sainsbury's, Sun-Pat, Waitrose, Whole Earth, Gales (but with hydrogenated oil and sugar) and Co-op (but with sugar).

Specialist peanut butters are also available from health-food shops. Not only are they free from additives but they may also be:

Salt and sugar free
Suma (crunchy or smooth)
Sunwheel (crunchy or smooth)

Whole Earth (crunchy or fine)
Green City (crunchy)
Neal's Yard (just peanut butter!)

Sugar free

Harvest (crunchy or smooth)
Granose (peanut butter or crumble)
Whole Earth (American-style – sweetened with apple juice – crunchy or smooth)

There are also other specialist nut butters and spreads from health-food shops:

Whole Earth 3 Nut Butter (peanuts, hazelnuts, almonds)
Suma Hazelnut Butter
Meridian Almond Butter

And instead of chocolate and nut spreads which usually contain dairy produce, vegetarians and vegans will be interested in carob and nut spreads such as: Western Isle, Carozel and Meridian Caronut.

POPCORN

Often a good alternative to sweets, popcorn is the kernel of maize – a whole grain. It can be 'popped' by placing in a saucepan with a tablespoonful of vegetable oil, putting over the heat with the lid on, and waiting until all the corn has expanded or popped. You can shake the pan to prevent the popcorn burning and then afterwards season it with salt or herbs or Marmite – or a little honey or melted carob. Ready-popped corn in different flavours, and the corn for popping at home, is available from health-food shops. Vegetarians can also buy bags of savoury popcorn from SunnyHill in the following flavours: Cheese, Savoury Butter and Paprika.

Microwave additive-free popcorn comes in a flat bag which explodes into life as the corn pops. The two brands are Hey Presto and Playtime DIY Poppers. Both are coated with hydrogenated vegetable oil but contain nothing else. Playtime also do a kit for traditional popcorn fans who like to make their popcorn in a saucepan. The bag contains a sachet of popcorn and a sachet of oil. You can, of course, just buy your own corn and oil. It's cheaper.

RICE

Rice is one of the most widely used grains and a major contributor of protein in half the world's diet. It is also important to vegetarians and vegans for its protein when it is used in combination with legumes and nuts and seeds.

Most of the world eats polished or refined white rice which has had the bran removed, along with some of the germ which contains vitamins and polyunsaturated oils. White rice is then polished and dusted with talc to improve its colour.

Brown rice retains most of the bran, for although milling removes the outer husk it leaves much of the bran and germ intact. These add fibre and vitamins to your diet. Brown rice does take longer to cook than white but it will usually be cooked in around thirty to thirty-five minutes. Short grain rice will cook quicker than long grain and although short grain is traditionally a pudding rice, either kind may be used in savoury paella, risotto, pillaus and other dishes.

Easy-cook or parboiled rice does not cook quicker than conventional brown rice but is more resistant to over-cooking. The rice is partially cooked under pressure before milling. This drives some vitamins and minerals from the husk into the grain, increasing, slightly, the nutritional value. It has a hardening effect on the grain.

Basmati brown rice from India is available for the connoisseur but much brown rice is now imported from America and Italy. Organic rice usually comes from Italy.

Wild rice is another grain for the gourmet, partly because it is very expensive. It is dark brown in colour, has a unique flavour and is not really a rice but a grass which grows around the Great Lakes in the United States. It is also high in fibre because it is unpolished.

An excellent canned convenience food from health-food shops is Whole Earth's Brown Rice and Vegetables which can be heated and served in one minute. Their rice is organically grown and has no additives.

Rice pudding

Can be made using short-grain brown rice with either skimmed milk or soya milk. But a quick-convenience soya milk rice-pudding for vegans is made by Granny Ann and Plamil and is available in cans from health-food shops.

SAUCES

Tomato ketchup and brown sauce are not quite ideal foods but they may be your particular weakness. If you do buy them, you may be interested in the ones that are free from additives and added sugar.

Tomato ketchup

<u>Whole Earth</u> sweetened with apple juice, but no added salt

<u>Life Low Sodium</u> sweetened with apple juice, contains honey, but no added salt

<u>Prewett's Low Sodium</u> sweetened with apple juice, but no added salt

Brown sauce

<u>HP</u> contains sugar and salt, but no animal products

<u>Life Low Sodium Fruity</u> no sugar, no salt, but does contain molasses

<u>Prewett's Low Sodium Spicy</u> no sugar, no salt, but does contain apple juice concentrate and molasses

<u>Whole Earth's Kensington</u> no sugar, sweetened with fruit juices, contains salt.

Other sauces

<u>Life Worcestershire</u> has no added salt or sugar and is free from animal products. Traditionally Worcestershire sauce contains anchovies, sugar and salt.

<u>Life Tartare</u> accompanies fish, but could be used elsewhere by vegetarians and vegans as it has no eggs and is high in poly-unsaturates.

<u>Life Horseradish</u> is another sauce used with meat and fish but this variety is free from added salt and sugar. It is acceptable to vegetarians, but not to vegans.

<u>Spaghetti Sauces</u> are tomato-based sauces for spaghetti. Some include meat in bolognese sauces, but others are just tomatoes, herbs and spices. Whole Earth Italiano! is acceptable to both vegetarians and vegans and is free from added sugar and salt.

Shoyu is the 'real' version of soya sauce, made of fermented soya-beans, wheat and salt.

Soya is often a cheap version of natural shoyu sauce containing additives such as MSG to enhance its flavour. Chemical additives used to speed the process do not allow the natural flavour of the slowly fermented shoyu to develop.

Tamari sauce is soya beans fermented by a bacteria starter. An even longer process than shoyu and tastes stronger. Contains no wheat.

SAUSAGES

Vegetarian sausages, of course. These are available frozen, fresh chilled or as dry packet mixes. Like vegetarian burgers, they are based on cereals, nuts and soya protein. Frying will add extra oil so they are best grilled or in casseroles. They may also be barbecued.

Vege Banger from Realeat (makers of the Vege Burger) are suitable for vegans and vegetarians and may be reconstituted from the dry packet mix with egg or water. Also available ready-made and frozen.

Haddington's kosher savoury or tomato sausages are free from animal products and based on soya protein. They are also available as sausage rolls in wholemeal pastry. All frozen.

Mr Chef vegetable and soya-based sausages are fresh chilled. They're not suitable for vegans because they contain milk protein.

Hera produce a vegetable soysage mix based on soya protein and cereal but which contains dairy products.

Boots vegetarian sausage mix.

SEEDS

Vegetarians and vegans can use sunflower, sesame and pumpkin seeds to add to their protein foods. Like nuts, seeds are a storehouse of vitamins and minerals that keep the plant alive until it has produced leaves to feed itself. They are also high in protein and can easily be added to muesli, breads, salads and burgers. You can also nibble them as snacks or instead of sweets but they are high in calories.

SOUP

Canned soups are a common store-cupboard stand-by for a quick, light meal, but you are more likely to find a dry, packet soup-mix that will satisfy vegetarian and vegan criteria. There is a range of additive and animal-free soups made by Hugli, a Swiss company, sold in health-food shops, where you will also find Prewett's and Hera soup-mixes which are all (except Hera Tomato) suitable for vegetarians and vegans.

In the High Street, Boots Second Nature packet soups are also additive-free and all except Green Rye Soup with Mushroom are suitable for vegetarians and vegans.

SPICES

Spices have strong and distinctive flavours and they are very useful for quick cooking because they can help you achieve flavours that are often associated with long, slow cooking. They should usually be put in at the beginning of cooking and sweated or sautéed with some of the other ingredients.

Kinds of spices

'Curry'-style – ground cumin, coriander, red pepper, paprika, garam masala, etc.

Sweet – cinnamon, cloves, nutmeg, allspice, ginger, etc.

Sweet and savoury – nutmeg, mace, ginger, etc.

A typical Caribbean mixture – cinnamon, cloves, allspice, pepper, paprika, cayenne, ginger

A typical Chinese mixture – star anise, Szechuan peppercorns, cinnamon, liquorice, ginger

STOCK

Essential for quick cooking and available as stock cubes or tubs of concentrates. However vegans do not fare well with stock cubes because most contain lactose (milk sugar). There are two that are free from lactose – Morga (standard and low sodium stock cubes) and

Lotus Brown Stock. Other stock cubes that are suitable for vegetarians are Hugli (standard and low sodium), Planataforce (no added salt) and Friggs. All are based on vegetable bouillons.

STUFFING

Usually used with poultry but there are packet mixes which vegetarians and vegans in a hurry might like to use as an accompaniment to other dishes. The Mr Harvey's Original range is based on wholemeal breadcrumbs with bran and is free from fat, additives, sugar and salt.

SUGAR

For the low-down on why you should be cutting down, see p. 13. If you do want sugar, you may be interested in unrefined sugars which are 'tastier' than white sugar and do have some traces of minerals and vitamins, although not enough to make a significant contribution to the diet.

Real, unrefined, raw cane sugars do have a flavour of their own and come in several varieties: Demerara, Muscovado and molasses. Other brown sugars may simply be dyed white sugar with no aroma or character.

Another option is the fruit sugar, fructose. It looks like white table sugar (sucrose) but has larger crystals and because it is sweeter you need not use so much. It is said to be less disruptive to blood-sugar levels than sucrose and that's why it's used in diabetic foods. You can use it in the same way as standard sugar.

SUNFLOWER SPREAD

Similar to tahini (below) but is made from crushing sunflower seeds (rather than sesame seeds) to a paste. It is available with or without added salt.

TAHINI

Like peanut butter, it is a useful high protein spread, but it is also high in calories from the oils in the sesame seeds. Five brands free from additives are Harmony, Sunwheel, Suma and Meridian (from health-food shops) and Cypressa (found in supermarkets). All can be used to make hummus (see 'Light Snacks and Salads' p. 125). Tahini is available in light (hulled seeds) and dark (unhulled seed). Some brands have added salt.

TEA

Tea, like coffee, is a stimulant, and the health-conscious vegetarian or vegan may like to try herb tea as an alternative, or certainly to replace some of the standard 'cuppas' during the day. There are several alternative teas such as:

Rooibos harvested in South Africa which has a very low tannin content. Tannin is acidic, may cause indigestion and can interfere with mineral absorption (p. 10).

Maté (or matte) is low in tannin and has less caffeine than standard black tea but more than herb teas. The tea is made from the leaves of a type of holly tree.

Decaffeinated tea is available from Luaka and St James's teas. They taste and look like standard teabags. Luaka is also available as loose tea in 125g packs.

WINE

You might think that all wines would be eminently suitable for vegetarians and vegans as they are just grapes fermented with yeast, but modern technology and some old practices, too, can involve animal products in the wine-making process.

Because there are no laws requiring alcoholic drinks to be labelled with a list of their ingredients, there is no way of knowing what is in, or has been used to make, your wine – this includes additives, too. You may wish, for example, to avoid wine that has been treated with egg-white, casein (milk protein), dried blood powder, animal albumins or sturgeon's air bladders to clarify it. The only way to find out if the treatments have been used is to write to the shipper, wine merchant, or the estate itself – a rather long-winded process.

Alternatively, you could go to a wine merchant who supplies

organic wines. As these wines do not have additives and as the makers pay special attention to ingredients and processing, you are more likely to find a 'vegetarian' wine. Some suppliers are:

The Organic Food Co. Ltd, PO Box 463, Portslade, Sussex BN4 1AJ (0273 424634).

Bibendum, 113 Regents Park Road, London NW1 8UR (01-586 9761). Minimum order one case (twelve bottles), with discount for collection.

Infinity Food Cooperative, 25 North Road, Brighton BN11YA (0273 424060). Minimum order one case. Can be bought by the bottle in the North Road shop.

Organic Farm Foods, Unit C, Hanworth Trading Estate, Hampton Road, West Feltham, Middlesex PW13 6DH.

West Heath Wines, West Heath, Pirbright, Surrey (04867 6464). Minimum order one case.

Wholefood, 24 Paddington Street, London W1M 4DR (01-935 3924). Buy by the bottle in the shop.

Roy Cooke, Pine Ridge Vineyards, Staplecross, Robertsbridge, East Sussex (015 083 715). Britain's first organic-wine producer who supplies his wine.

The Lincolnshire Wine Company, Chapel Lane, Ludborough, near Grimsby (0472 840858), twenty-four-hour telephone service and free delivery within thirty miles of Louth. German wines only.

The Organic Wine Company Ltd, PO Box 81, High Wycombe, Bucks. HP11 1LJ (0494 446557). Mainly French wines.

YEAST EXTRACTS

These are very useful for vegetarians and vegans because they are enriched with vitamin B_{12} (p. 11). They can be added to stocks, soups, etc. while cooking or used as a savoury spread for sandwiches and toast. There are several brands available in health-food shops including Natex, Barmene and Tastex. In the supermarket you will find Marmite and possibly even Vegemite, the Australian equivalent of Marmite.

THE VEGETARIAN FRIDGE AND FREEZER

As a vegetarian aiming for a healthy diet, you are going to need a good-sized fridge for all the fresh fruit and vegetables that will make up a significant part of your intake. The ideal is a large salad tray, together with deep shelves and trays in the fridge doors for cartons and bottles of fruit and vegetable juice, skimmed milk and soya milk.

Although you will not have the problems of keeping meat and fish fresh, alternative sources of protein such as dairy products and tofu also need to be kept in a chilled environment. If you sprout your own seeds, these can be stored in the fridge in their tiered trays to slow growth or they can be transferred to clean polythene bags when they have reached the required size.

Bread and yeasted items can also be kept fresher during warm weather in a fridge – if you have the space. You can also store left-over brewed coffee or other drinks and keep your beer on ice . . .

With the increasing range of convenience ready-meals for vegetarians and vegans in health-food shops, supermarkets and High Street chains, you will also be able to make good use of a freezer. Any gluts of fresh fruit and vegetables can be frozen.

Specialist non-dairy iced desserts are also now available but you may find that you prefer to make your own as there is still a limited choice in the shops. Baking in batches is most economical and a freezer makes storage possible. Longer-cooking items such as beans, pulse-based curries and hotpots can also be cooked in batches and frozen.

BEER

Unlike wine, beer will not have been treated with any animal-derived additives or processing aids, but it may contain some of the many additives allowed in modern brewing. There are no laws requiring ingredients to be listed (although some beers do list them) so to find out the ingredients you will have to ask the brewery.

BURGERS

Frozen

These may be fried or grilled from frozen. They are based on soya proteins, cereal, rusks and dried vegetables and flavoured with herbs and spices. They are available from health-food shops and a few supermarket chains stock them in some of their branches. Some brands are:

Vege Burgers from Realeat, the most widely available. Also available as Cheese Vege Burger

Sunrise from Soya Health Foods

Nutriburger from Care Foods

No Meat Grill Burgers from Haddington's.

Fresh chilled

These are mainly found in the cold cabinets of health-food and wholefood shops. These are mostly based on tofu, the curd made from soya milk in a process similar to cheesemaking. Tofu is popular in Japanese cooking and is called beancurd on Chinese restaurant menus. It is virtually fat-free and high in protein. Kinds to look out for are:

Paul's Tofu tofu burgers in curry, herby and nutty varieties

Soyboy tofu burgers in savoury herb and chilli varieties

Cauldron Foods in vegetable, chilli and nut varieties

Tofeata tofu burgers from Hera, spicy and savoury burgers, plus Okara Patties. Okara is a high-fibre bulk left after making soya milk from soya beans.

CHEESE

Cheese is an especially convenient food for vegetarians (although not for vegans) and one easy to eat too much of because it is more-ish, versatile and provides protein. As we have seen (p. 13), it is a high-fat food and so it is best used in moderation. In China, Japan and India many generations of vegetarians have lived quite healthily without it. To continue to enjoy it, the healthiest way is to cut out the nibbles and to use it as a main ingredient.

Vegetarian cheese

Special vegetarian rennet is available to cheesemakers so they can clot the milk without having to use rennin, the enzyme taken from the stomach of slaughtered calves, which does the job in most cheese. Vegetarian agents for clotting milk are plant or fungi enzymes or lactic acid and bacteria. Most large supermarkets now stock own-brand or other vegetarian cheese, and health-food and wholefood shops have traditionally done so. The main brands of vegetarian cheese are:

Marigold Cheddar, Cheshire, Dutch Gouda

Prewett's Cheddar, Cheshire, Bleasdale, Wensleydale, Double Gloucester, Lancashire

Farm Maid Cheddar, Cheshire, Double Gloucester, Red Leicester, Wensleydale

St Ivel Cheddar.

Other vegetarian cheeses

Naturally low-fat cheeses are made from skimmed milk and they do not use rennet. Instead the milk is curdled into curds and whey, using bacteria or lactic acid.

	Fat content (%)
Cottage cheese – made from skimmed milk	2 – 4
Ricotta – made from whole and skimmed milk	5 – 10
Curd cheeses – as above	5 – 10
Quark – made from skimmed milk	5 – 10
Lebne (Lebna/Lebnie) – a strained yoghurt	5 – 10
Skimmed milk soft cheese	5 – 10

Cottage cheese often contains preservatives. Additive-free varieties are available in health-food shops and some delicatessens. Eden Vale and Marks & Spencer's natural cottage cheese are free from additives.

Low-fat cheese

There are several types of low-fat cheese available, usually of the more popular traditional hard cheeses. They have about half the fat (15 per cent) of standard cheeses, but only one is made with vegetarian rennet – Prewett's reduced-fat vegetarian cheese, which is 15 per cent fat and cheddar-style.

Special cheese

One cheese offers the unusual attraction of being high in polyunsaturates (most cheeses are virtually totally saturated) – Soderasens Vegetarian Vegetable Oil Cheese. It is made in the same way as conventional cheese but it mixes skimmed pasteurized milk with sunflower and soya oils. There are two varieties, standard and vegetarian, available from health-food shops and supermarkets.

Rennet

If you want to make your own hard or soft cheese, vegetarian rennet is sold in health-food shops or from the specialist cheese equipment suppliers, R. J. Fullwood & Bland Ltd, Rennet Works, Ellesmere, Shropshire (069 171 2391).

Additives

Most cheeses are made without additives and use natural, traditional processes. Cheddar, Cheshire, Leicester, etc. do not contain additives and even though sorbic acid is allowed, it is not usually used. However, Edam and Gouda do contain sodium nitrite and sodium nitrate (E250 and E251). Processed cheeses and flavoured cheese-spreads are made by heating cheese and then blending – sometimes with the addition of flavourings – emulsifying agents, lactic and acetic acids.

EGGS

There are many humanitarian arguments against the battery system which does not allow hens to behave naturally or to exercise and which leads to aggression and fighting among the birds. From the health point of view, drugs are necessary to keep hens 'healthy' under these conditions and colourings are used in their feed to make the pallid yolks uniformly yellow.

The alternative is free-range hens which produce eggs that contain more B vitamins than battery eggs and may have other nutritional advantages not yet monitored by scientific tests. The chickens have day-time access to open-air runs. Semi-intensive eggs come from hens with the same access, but less space. Deep-litter eggs are from hens that live indoors and have less space than free-range but more than semi-intensive. Perchy or barn eggs are from indoor hens which live in far more crowded conditions than the previous categories, but have allocated additional space on perches.

So ignore all the 'country fresh', 'farm eggs' selling-hype on the boxes and look for the above official terms if you want to buy eggs from a system other than the battery one.

FRUIT (AND VEGETABLES)

As vegetarians and vegans you will be buying and eating more fresh fruit and vegetables than your meat-eating friends. Because they are an important part of your diet, you will want to find a good supplier whether a local supermarket, market, greengrocer or health-food shop.

Health-food shops might seem an odd choice to you but more and more are supplying organically grown fresh produce. The advantage of organic produce is that it is grown without the use of chemical fertilizers and without chemical treatments such as pesticides, herbicides and then fungicides to treat the harvested produce and its wrappers.

There is a recognized symbol for produce grown to the standards of the Soil Association, the original organization in Britain to recognize organic needs and lay down the standards for growers. The Soil Association monitors farms and awards growers the use of the symbol when they have reached its standards.

The overall regulatory body in the UK is the British Organic Standards Committee (BOSB), which was formed in 1980 with members from the Soil Association and other groups of organic growers and experts. Each of the organizations involved in organics

puts its standards before B O S B for approval, which means there are several different symbols and slightly different systems in operation. Above is a pictorial guide to the ones to look out for.

Organic farming also promotes a sustainable system that does not pollute the soil and waterways with chemicals. It offers a healthier prospect for you, for the future of the environment and ultimately, grandiose though it may sound, for the survival of the planet!

* Not quite the same criteria as organic but similar.

Specialist stockists

Wholefood, 24 Paddington Street, London W1M 4DR, is a wholefood shop with an organic greengrocer and an organic butcher in the same street.

Infinity Foods Cooperative, 25 North Row, Brighton BN1 1YA, stocks a complete range of organic foods and is also an organic wholesaler and distributor with a cash-and-carry at 67 Norway Street, Portslade, East Sussex BN4 1AE.

Neal's Yard, Covent Garden, London WC1, stocks organic fruit and vegetables, plus general produce.

Beehive Restaurant and Shop, 11a Beehive Place, Brixton, London SW9, stocks fruit and vegetables, bread, dairy produce and baby food.

Your local health-food or wholefood shop will have some organic products.

FRUIT JUICE

This is a type of drink that vegetarians and vegans can feel confident will not contain any animal products. From the health-conscious shopper's view there are a few points to watch out for.

First, make sure the carton says 'juice' and not 'drink'. Although they all look similar with pictures of fruit, there is a difference. 'Drinks' contain water, sugar and possibly colourings, preservatives, etc. Fruit 'nectars' contain added water and sugar and may contain additives. Juice may be made from concentrates or freshly squeezed juice, or a combination of the two. Natural preservatives such as vitamin C (citric acid), lactic and malic acid are allowed in some juices – the ingredients list will indicate if they have been used.

Some juices made from concentrates are reconstituted with spring water or demineralized water rather than local tap waters, which juice producers in this country use. Tap water in certain areas contains added fluoride. Stute and Volonte juices are, respectively, spring and demineralized water.

Aspall and Copella apple juices are made in Britain from organically produced fruit. Health-food shops stock other imported organic juices.

GARLIC

Garlic is essential for flavoursome vegetarian and vegan dishes. Choose dry, papery bulbs containing moist, fleshy cloves without mould. Try to avoid any garlic that is sprouting or green as the flavour may be bitter.

GINGER

Fresh root ginger will keep well in the fridge and is very handy to have for Chinese, Indian, Malaysian or Thai-style dishes. It grates easily and imparts flavour quickly. It is also good for hot drinks.

ICE-CREAM

Until recently vegans could not enjoy ice-cream, very much a dairy-based product, but new alternatives to ice-cream based on soya mean that vegans who do eat honey can now join in summer treats. By law, ice-cream has to contain cows'-milk products so the alternatives have to be called something other than ice-cream.

Scrummi Iced Confection is made by Vegetarian Feasts and contains tofu (p. 79), honey and fruit whipped together to make 'ice-cream'.

Sojal Frozen Desserts are made from soya milk sweetened with honey, polyunsaturated vegetable oils, natural flavours, soya lecithin (a natural emulsifier) and guar gum.

Sunrise Soya Milk Ice Dream is made from soya milk, corn syrup solids, soya bean oil, fructose, vanilla, vegetable gums and natural colours.

Vive Frozen Desserts from Allied Foods Ice-Cream Company is made from sugar, coconut oil, modified starch, glucose syrup, soya protein isolate, fruit and cocoa or carob. The stabilizers used are vegetable gums.

Dayvilles N'ice Day is made by Dayvilles of ice-cream parlour fame. It is based on soya milk, raw cane sugar, corn syrup, vegetable oil (palm), soya protein, natural flavour, natural stabilizer (guar and carob gum), lecithin and natural colouring.

For vegetarians there are some 'healthier' ice-creams, such as:

Loseley Ice-no-Cream made from skimmed milk with passion fruit and brown sugar.

Milk Ice from Blackburne & Haynes is made from skimmed milk and fruit. All the varieties except blackcurrant are free from additives.

At the other extreme are luxury ice-creams which are generally additive-free but may contain eggs and do contain cream so they are higher in saturated fat than standard ice-creams.

Loseley Dairy Ice Cream contains 21 per cent double cream, raw cane sugar and natural flavours.

Blackburne & Haynes and Cricketer St Thomas make similar ice-creams.

Wall's have also produced an 'all-natural' range, but vegetarians might not want to buy it because it contains gelatine.

One possible ice lolly for vegans is to be found in the Co-op Natural Ice Lolly range. Of four lollies in the range one, Little Menace Orange, is free from dairy produce, but all lollies contain saccharine.

MARGARINE

Vegetarians may choose to use butter sometimes but vegans will only use margarines that are free from animal products. You may also prefer soft vegetable margarines that are high in polyunsaturates (see discussion of fats, p. 7).

Vegan margarine

Vitaquell range from health-food shops is made with cold-pressed vegetable oils and is the only range that does not use any hydrogenated vegetable oils. Instead of chemically hardening the oils to get a spreading texture, they are blended with naturally firm oils such as palm oil. The range is free from all animal ingredients and high in polyunsaturates.

Prewett's sunflower and safflower margarines are high in polyunsaturates and free from animal products.

Granose vegetable margarine in the green pack is high in polyunsaturates (the red pack is not) and free from animal products.

Suma is a health-food wholesaler and shop in Leeds. Their sunflower margarine is high in polyunsaturates and free from animal products.

Tomar is a kosher margarine which is free from all animal products and very low in polyunsaturates.

Vegan cooking fats

White Flora is 100 per cent vegetable fat and is unusual among cooking fats in being high in polyunsaturates and free from animal products.

Vegetable Suet and Nut Butters are not recommended because they are hydrogenated hard fats and thus saturated. They may be animal-free but they won't help change the ratio of fats in your diet (p. 7).

Vegetarian margarine

To the above list of margarines, vegetarians could add the following which are high in polyunsaturates but which contain whey or skimmed-milk powder, making them unavailable to vegans.

Flora – whey

Gold Cup – whey, whey solids

Kraft Vitalite – as above

Marks & Spencer Sunflower – reconstituted dried whey, dried whey

Safeway Sunflower – whey (also sugar). Also in salt-free version.

Sainsbury's Sunflower – reconstituted whey powder

Waitrose Sunflower Soft – whey (also sugar)

Gateway Sunflower – whey. Also in salt-free version.

MAYONNAISE AND SALAD CREAM

By law these have to contain vegetable oil and egg – the latter makes them out of bounds for vegans. They may also contain a lot of additives, sugar and salt. To get round this problem, mayonnaise-style dressings have been produced and these are the ones for vegans (and vegetarians) to look out for. Vegans can usually buy French and Italian vinaigrette-style dressings.

Vegans

Whole Earth Creamy Nut Dressing is made from peanuts and is dairy-free with no added sugar or salt.

Prewett's Low Sodium Mayonnaise-style Salad Dressing and Salad Cream, although marketed for their low sodium content, are of interest to vegans because they are entirely animal-free.

Life Mayonnaise-style Sunflower/Salad-cream-style Dressings are dairy-free vegan dressings with no added salt or sugar.

<u>Life Salad Cream-style Dressing</u> is free from additives and eggs.

<u>Duchesse French/Sunflower/Tofu/Garlic/Avocado/Thousand Island/
Italian Dressings</u> are high in polyunsaturates and low in salt.

<u>Tofu Soyannaise</u> is mayonnaise-style but animal-free and based on
tofu. It does contain honey and the additives used are all natural
plant derivatives.

Vegetarians

To the above vegan shopping list, vegetarians can add real mayon-
naise products. These are more expensive than products made from
oil and eggs but they are free from additives and more like the real
thing. The ones without additives are:
  Kite Wholefoods (also sold as Suma) Mayonnaise
  Ratcliffe's Real Mayonnaise
  Safeway Real/Garlic/Lemon/Mustard Mayonnaise
  Cuisine Real Mayonnaise.

<u>Proper Mayonnaise</u> is produced from fresh eggs, olive oil and wine
vinegar and is made by the traditional chef's method. From
delicatessens and health-food shops in the South.

<u>Suma Mayonnaise</u> is another traditional, real mayonnaise from
health-food shops in the North.

READY-MEALS

Fresh chilled

There are a growing number of convenience meals for vegetarians,
some of which are based on wholefood principles. These quick dishes
can be bought from major multiples or from health-food and
wholefood shops. They're very handy for the vegetarian fridge and
freezer.
  Some of the main brands are mentioned below.

<u>St Michael</u> range of recipe dishes include vegetable- and pasta-based
meals. The cheese used is vegetarian but the meals are not
'wholefood' although most are free from additives.

Waitrose ready meals include some cheese-based vegetable dishes that are suitable for vegetarians but are not wholefood.

Spaghetti House and Pasta Reale have ready-made meals and fresh pasta with sauces, many of which are suitable for vegetarians and free from additives and colourings.

Frozen

Vegetarian Feasts have the most extensive range of wholefood vegetarian meals from everyday dishes to more exotic ones for dinner or entertaining.

Realeat have a range of everyday vegetarian meals based on pasta and lentils and made to wholefood criteria.

St Nicholas Wholefoods, as the name suggests, base their pies and casserole-style dishes on wholefood ingredients like wholemeal pastry.

Capricorn offer a good range of main courses, including pizza and pasta dishes, plus some good family-favourite desserts.

Vege-dine have a wide wholefood range of popular pasta, curry, casserole and pie dishes that make good use of nuts and grains.

Whole Faire are a smaller wholefood company offering basic frozen curry, crumble and chilli dishes.

Bird's Eye single-serving but not wholefood vegetarian meals in their Menu Master range.

SOYA MILK

Soya milk has been used for centuries in China and Japan as dairy produce was once unheard of there. The milk is made by boiling ground soya beans in water and straining off the milky liquid that results. Sometimes a sweetener such as sugar or barley malt is added and maybe salt too. Soya milk is high in protein and very low in fat, but does not contain the calcium found in cows' milk (for discussion of calcium see pp. 8–10). You can use soya milk on cereals, in drinks and for cooking or to make yoghurts and ice-creams. Most varieties are UHT and packed in cartons so they are long life but, once opened, need to be refrigerated and used within a few days in the same way that dairy milk does.

The main brands free from additives are:

Provamel, made by Granose who produce a sugar-free soya milk and soya milk 'drinks' which contain honey and are flavoured with carob or strawberry

Plamil, the first British soya milk producer

Sunrise, a UHT long-life milk available with or without added sugar

Sojal, no added sugar or salt

Prewett's, sweetened with honey

Itona, in cans and sweetened with raw cane sugar

Eden and Bonsoy, imported from Japan and in sachet/pouches in individual servings as plain or flavoured. No added sugar.

Buying soya milk:

- remember some varieties have added sugar, so check that the brand is sugar-free
- read the ingredients panel for additives although soya milk is usually free from them as it's sold, at the moment, mainly through health-food stores
- check the several flavoured soya milks on the market – most of which are of natural origin – to see if they have added sugar and colouring, etc.
- watch out for claims about being sugar-free or free from added sugar. While this may be true, the product may contain added malt, honey or sugar in another of its disguises.

Storing soya milk

If you haven't used it before, here are some tips on keeping soya milk:
- do not dilute concentrated soya milk until the moment of use. Leave the rest undiluted.
- do not cover the carton or can once opened to exclude the air.

This 'incubates' the milk and reduces keeping time. Allow it to breathe.

- do not store opened milk in a can. Pour into a non-metallic container.
- once opened put in the fridge – it will keep there for about five days.

SPROUTED SEEDS

Most people think seeds are only for planting in the garden but you can sprout seeds to make interesting vegetable and salad items. Eating seeds, you are taking advantage of nature's storehouse of food from which the germinating plant grows. That's why seeds are high in protein and vegetable oils which contain vitamin E. They are also good sources of B vitamins, vitamin A, magnesium, zinc, some iron and phosphorus.

Lots of seeds and beans can be successfully sprouted. The seeds include alfalfa, sesame and sunflower; and the beans for sprouting are adzuki, black-eye, chickpea, mung and soya. Just soak the seeds or beans you are using for several hours, drain and then water daily for four to five days (see Salad Sprouter p. 88). Eat the seeds raw but lightly cook the beans before eating.

SORBET

(See also, *Ice-cream*.)
Is often lower in calories than ice-cream and although traditionally made with egg-whites it can be commercially produced without them. There are a few additive-free sorbets suitable for vegetarians and vegans.

Loseley – real fruit, brown sugar, water, glucose solids, skimmed milk powder, Jersey double cream, citric acid and vegetable gum.

Wall's Alpine – real fruit, but lots of sugar and glucose syrup, plus natural gums and flavours.

Prospero fruit purées sweetened with fruit juice and set with pectin.

TOFU

Tofu is made by coagulating soya milk into a curd and draining off the water in the same way we make cheese from dairy milk. It is sold in small blocks which are prepacked and can be used in Oriental-style stir-fry dishes or made into burgers and cheesecakes. It has very little flavour and does not dominate dishes. It is also useful for low-calorie salad dressings.

Tofu is mostly sold as a long-life product in vacuum packs or in cartons but there are also fresh-chilled vacuum packs of plain and smoked tofu from manufacturers in this country. Once open, tofu will keep in the fridge for about seven days if stored in chilled water, changed daily.

Morinaga silken tofu is imported from Japan and is a long-life product sold in cartons. It is pasteurized but free from preservatives.

Tofeata is available from the Hera label endorsed by the Chinese chef Ken Lo and is vacuum-packed in a pouch inside a carton. The pack has several recipe ideas to get you started if tofu is new to you.

Cauldron Foods sell vacuum-packed tofu with a long shelf-life. It is packed in see-through pouches inside smart well-designed cartons and is available in plain and smoked versions.

Paul's Tofu is another chilled and vacuum-packed product in a see-through container sold in health-food shops.

YOGHURT

Yoghurt is one of the original 'health foods' as plain (natural) yoghurt is just milk fermented by bacteria. For the vegetarian there are other considerations.

First, if you are cutting down on fat (see discussion of fats p. 7) you will want to choose yoghurts labelled:

	Fat content (%)
Low fat	0.5–2%
Very low fat	less than 0.5%
Skimmed milk	less than 0.5%

You will also want 'live' yoghurt which contains the beneficial bacteria that can produce B vitamins in the gut. All yoghurts should be 'live' even if the tub does not say so, unless they are long-life or sterilized yoghurts that have been heat-treated after they have been made.

To avoid the very sugary yoghurts or those containing artificial additives read the ingredients list or panel. And if you want a yoghurt with real fruit in it, it will be labelled: strawberry or strawberry-flavoured. If the flavour is artificial, it will say: strawberry flavour.

There are several brands that are free from additives, low in fat and contain real fruit. They are:

St Ivel
Chambourcy Nouvelle, Bonjour, Robot
Loseley
Holland & Barrett, raw sugar and sugar-free

Try your health-food shops for local dairies' additive-free yoghurts or for goat's and sheep's milk yoghurt.

Other yoghurt

Greek (or Greek-style) yoghurt is higher in fat than standard yoghurt — around 10 per cent — and it is usually made from cows' milk. It is popular because it is thick and creamy. The consistency is achieved by straining the yoghurt to remove the watery part, after which it is often heat-treated for longer shelf-life and so is not usually 'live'.

Vegan yoghurt

Yoghurt has to be made from dairy milk so the manufacturers of soya yoghurt (which uses soya milk) have had to come up with other names for their products available from health-food shops.

Sojal Yoga is made by Haldane Foods and is available in real fruit varieties.

Sunrise Soya Milk Low Fat Yoghurt does use the name 'yoghurt'.

Equipping the Vegetarian Kitchen

This guide assumes you have basic kitchen items such as a cooker, fridge, kettle, toaster, china, cutlery and glasses. It looks at the equipment you will be using to process food before cooking.

Key   *** *essential*
         ** *jolly useful*
         * *worth thinking about*

ALUMINIUM FOIL

Aluminium foil should not, in my opinion, be in direct contact with food, especially for cooking. It can still be useful for wrapping cakes and sandwiches but with a layer of greaseproof paper between the food and the foil. (See discussion of aluminium in SAUCEPANS.)

BALLOON WHISK ***

If you don't have an electric-mixer or processor, then a balloon whisk is vital for whisking egg-whites or batters. It gives the quickest results of all hand-whisks and is easiest to clean. It is also more effective for whisking a single egg-white. Balloon whisks are usually made of metal but birch ones can be left in sauces in the microwave during cooking.

BLENDER/LIQUIDIZER ***

If you don't have one on your food processor or with your mixer, then this is a valuable investment for soups and desserts, purées and sauces. Sometimes curdled items respond, if caught soon enough, to a whiz in the blender.

BREADBOARD ***

On a high-fibre diet you might be aiming to eat four slices of wholemeal bread a day and inevitably you will graduate to 'real' bread that needs slicing. Cutting your own loaf means thicker slices – eating more bread and less of the filling. It makes sense to have an attractive breadboard that you can use at the table and which is also more hygienic than using the chopping-board.

CAN-OPENER ***

Vital! Forget the old can-openers that you dig into the can and jerk around the edge. Choose one with a butterfly nut that will whiz round the top of the can. The MagiCan version is probably best because it takes off the whole top of the can so you don't risk cut fingers and thumbs when you prise up the lid.

CHOPPING-BOARD ***

This is essential for a vegetarian who will be chopping, dicing and slicing quantities of fresh fruits and vegetables. Either buy two chopping-boards or choose a reversible one so that you can use one side for vegetables, garlic and chillies and the other side for fruits and sweet items – unless, of course, you like a garlic-tainted fruit salad!

Wooden chopping-boards can harbour bacteria in cracks and cuts but as you will not be putting meat or fish on to the board it is unlikely that you will be at risk from salmonella bacteria which cause food-poisoning – provided you scrub a wooden board after use and don't leave it soaking in water. Another material used for chopping-boards is marble which is very expensive, heavy and stains easily. A synthetic material made to resemble marble is Corian, smooth, heavy and hardwearing (available from David Mellor). Synthetic patterned boards are not really pleasing to work on as they crack and chip easily and the top layer often lifts off.

CLINGFILM

Clingfilm is controversial because its possibly carcinogenic molecules may 'wander' into food. You can use either a 'safe' brand such as Glad Wrap (not as clinging as other brands) or make sure it is not in direct contact with food – especially oily or fatty foods like meat and cheese. I use it over the top of basins containing food, where it acts as a seal and prevents two-way taint. Do *not* use it in the microwave oven because it causes most contamination of food in this situation.

COLANDER * *

Stainless steel colanders are expensive but they last for a long time and clean easily, whereas plastic colanders can become cracked and harbour germs, melt or even cause a fire if left too near the hob.

EGG-SLICER *

It might seem an extravagance for vegetarian cooking but garnishing is important. An egg-slicer is also handy for sandwiches (open sandwiches too) and salads as it makes quick work of a fiddly job.

FOOD PROCESSOR/MIXER * * *

If you do not already own either of these, then you must weigh up their pros and cons and decide which would suit your needs best.

If you are very tight for space then you may opt for a food processor. The advantage is that most have fewer and smaller 'extras' than a mixer, so they need less storage space. Whichever you choose, you will want to keep it out on the worksurface so it is easy to get to; both are too heavy to keep lifting in and out of cupboards. A dust-cover is essential. You may be able to throw away a lot of other equipment once you have a processor, but there are times when you will need or want to do things by hand.

I think a mixer (the Kenwood Chef Excel, for example) is the best buy because it gives much better results for baking and bread-making and it can cope with larger (and smaller) quantities of food than the processors. It also has some very valuable optional extras that do jobs the food processor can't. Adding the extras is cheaper than buying, for example, a pasta machine and a juicer: the pasta maker can produce tagliatelle noodles, spaghetti and macaroni; the juicer produces pulp and juice. Other extras include the very useful coffee grinder, a wheatmill which allows you to make your own flour (using grains and pulses) and a citrus juice extractor. The slicer, shredder and liquidizer do all the jobs a food processor can do.

The mincer is possibly extraneous to vegetarian needs, as is the potato peeler, but the bean-slicer could be valuable if you cope with gluts of garden produce.

FORK ***

A good-sized fork is necessary for mixing dough, cakes, pancake mixes and batters.

FRUIT SQUEEZER ***

A hand-size one is very useful for the odd half-lemon or orange (or even for breakfast drinks) when you don't want to use the liquidizer or juicer. One with a tray that collects the pulp and lets the juice strain through to the base is recommended. Make sure it has a good pouring lip.

GARLIC PRESS **

This is vital. Don't bother with a pestle and mortar because it will likely become tainted and it takes longer than using a garlic press. Make sure it's firm and has a handle that's easy to grip.

GRATER **

For small quantities of vegetables and cheese, a hand-held grater is quicker than using the food processor. A square stainless steel one is easiest to use because it contains the grated food within the square and doesn't spray it all over the worktop or out of the bowl into which you are grating. It will also have a choice of grating blades – rough, smooth and very fine for nutmeg. Scrub it clean with a brush after use.

GREASEPROOF PAPER ***

Ideal for wrapping foods for cooking and for refrigeration. For example, cheese can be wrapped with clingfilm outside the grease-proof paper to seal it. It is also useful for lining cake tins and baking trays and for putting on top of items in the oven to prevent over-browning.

KNIVES * * *

Food preparation will be quicker if you have the right tools for the job and a selection of different sizes of knife will help. For example, a small vegetable knife will allow you to chop onions quicker than a large heavy knife which will chop up a large swede efficiently.

Knives should be kept sharp because they are then easier to use. More accidents are caused by applying extra pressure to 'blunt' knives which then slip and cause cuts. Store sharp knives in the cardboard or plastic sheaths in which they were sold or in a knife-block or magnetic rack.

Stainless steel knives are easiest to maintain because they do not rust. Check that the handle fits well and has no crevices where food can accumulate along with bacteria.

Modern laser knives have stainless steel edges cut by laser and are said not to need sharpening for twenty-five years. Other stainless steel knives will need to be sharpened – have it done professionally or buy a steel. Sabatier knives are made by licensed manufacturers in and around Sabatier in France and have an excellent reputation.

Choose a good range of knives such as these: vegetable knife, small cook's knife, parer, larger cook's knife, grapefruit knife, bread knife. The money you save on a meat cleaver and carving set you can invest in other knives of your choice.

MASHER * *

You don't have to like mashed potato to find a potato masher useful. It will start off the mashing of many items which can then be transferred to the liquidizer or food processor, or it will do the whole job. It is also handy for small portions if there is a baby in the house.

MEASURING JUG * * *

This saves disasters when cooking as it cuts out the guesswork. It can double up as a storage vessel for the fridge and for pouring liquids into containers. Use it in conjunction with a small funnel which might seem fussy but saves time in the long run because you make less mess and have less waste. Make sure the jug has a good pouring lip.

MICROWAVE *

Some people are still suspicious of microwave ovens, but provided they are properly maintained it seems to me that there is no real evidence against them. They can cook vegetables and vegetarian dishes quickly and cleanly, they cut down on washing up and they are versatile. As long as they are not used to supply a diet of reheated convenience foods, I think there is room for one in a busy vegetarian's kitchen. They are bulky items but I don't think it is worth buying the smallest one as the oven space is very limited. Neither do I think the pre-programmed versions are worth spending extra on.

Choose one with a wide range of power settings and then use it as you would the oven or hob, making your own judgement about how long to cook things for, after taking initial guidance from the manufacturer's instruction book. This way the microwave oven becomes a useful tool in quickly making sauces, for example, and in preparing fruit and vegetables for your own dishes and recipes.

Although microwaves save time on most foods, they will not cut down on the cooking time for dried beans and other pulses or for items such as dried chestnuts or pasta. For these you need to top up the water in the microwave oven more often than for quicker-cooking foods.

MICROWAVE COOKWARE

Choose specialist microwave ovenware or Pyrex (or similar glass) or ceramic items *with lids* as then you will not have to use clingfilm (see p. 82). Check that the glass or ceramic ware does not heat up but allows the microwaves through to heat the food. You can also use these items for conventional cooking and so cut down on finding extra storage space for microwave cookware.

MIXING BOWL * * *

I have found it easiest to have a spare mixing bowl for my Kenwood Chef and then use the two bowls as general-purpose mixing bowls. Handy when, for example, you are creaming a mixture and then want to add whisked egg whites. You just slip another bowl under the whisk and then off you go without stopping to wash up. They are also good-sized deep bowls which allow you to introduce plenty of air when rubbing in fat and flour.

PASTRY BRUSH **

This is useful for glazing pastry and other baked items. It is also handy for greasing cake tins, moulds and baking trays and for oiling saucepans and frying pans because you will use less oil than if you tipped the bottle by hand. Be careful if oiling hot pans – your brush might melt.

PEELER *

Although in most cases you will be eating fruits and vegetables with the skins on, there will be times when you need a peeler for vegetables such as swede or fruits like kiwi fruit. One with a built-in apple-corer is ideal, but make sure it has a comfortable handle.

PESTLE AND MORTAR *

This is not essential but jolly useful if you like using spices for savoury, sweet or ethnic dishes such as Indian, Thai, etc. (see 'Special-occasion Menus' p. 181). You can mix your own 'curry powders' and blend items like chillies, ginger, garlic and lemon grass into marinating pastes. I use a science lab, solid stone pestle and mortar. It's heavier, therefore very stable, and more effective than marble or wood which don't cope as well with hard spices and which don't have a 'grip' on their smooth surfaces. It also cleans well.

PLASTIC CONTAINERS/BASINS ***

Choose either/or for storing food in the fridge – any remains of opened cans or left-over vegetables, fruit, salad – but don't keep cheese or vegetables in them. Put these in the salad tray and door sections in the fridge. I prefer to use ceramic basins with clingfilm over the top (*not* in contact with the food) because this avoids picking up food taints. But you might find plastic containers useful if you keep specific ones for specific jobs. For example, you could keep one (with a lid) in the fridge for left-over stock/gravy/vegetable water (not cabbage or potato), which you can then use for making soups and casseroles. I also find it useful to have a container for coffee as it's wasteful to throw away unused coffee from the percolator or coffee-filter machine. Soon after it's made, pour the coffee you aren't drinking into a storage jug (with a lid) and then reheat the coffee in the microwave (better than boiling it on the hob) or use it in desserts/cakes, etc.

PRESSURE COOKER *

If you cook beans and other dried pulses and hard vegetables, such as beetroot and swede, on a regular basis you will find a pressure cooker very useful. If you have a microwave you might not need a pressure cooker, but it cannot cook pulses as quickly as a pressure cooker. Choose a stainless steel cooker (see argument against aluminium in SAUCEPANS) and follow the manufacturer's instructions. Pressure cookers allow you to cook at two or three pressures and the instruction booklets give tables of cooking times so you don't overcook vegetables. More sophisticated models have built-in timers which warn you when food is ready.

ROLLING PIN **

Fancy ones which contain water and those with handles are unnecessary. A simple, good-weight rolling pin is all that is required. Paint won't chip off the handles and with your hands directly on the rolling pin and not on the handles you are better able to control what you are doing.

SALAD SPROUTER *

Sprouting seeds and beans (p. 78) is a cheap way of producing a salad, especially when ingredients are scarce or expensive in the winter. Salad sprouters are two or three tiers of perforated trays with a saucer tray at the base to catch drips. Seeds are soaked and then watered daily until they have sprouted sufficiently to be added to salads and other dishes.

SAUCEPANS ***

I find it invaluable to have two types of saucepan – good quality stainless steel with well-fitting lids and heavy cast-iron Le Creuset pans. Stainless steel may be expensive but the saucepans last for ever, are easy to clean and look good. They are ideal for fruit and vegetables because they do not react chemically as aluminium pans do to deposit minute amounts of metal in food. Neither do they become as pitted or marked as aluminium pans if acidic food is cooked in them. Aluminium is thought to contribute to Alzheimer's Disease (premature senility) – in Britain saucepans are considered a likely source of this aluminium.

The heavier cast-iron pans are ideal for cooking on the hob because they conduct heat so well that they need only a low setting on electricity or gas. They also allow food without additional liquid (nutritionally useful) to cook without burning or sticking to the pan. If you buy the black range (not enamel-lined), it also has handles that allow pans to be transferred easily from hob to oven. If I had only one saucepan it would be the Marmetout – a deep saucepan with a lid that doubles as an omelette pan/crêpe maker/frying pan/gratin dish and also transfers to the oven. Choose pans for small quantities of food as well as larger ones for cooking rice, pasta or beans.

SCALES ***

These cut out the guesswork in cooking. Choose scales with a good-size container that is also marked with liquid measures. I prefer the jug-type container to the ordinary pan because it is handy for pouring. However, the quickest way of using scales is to put the item – for example, a jar of honey or tub of margarine – into the scale pan and measure the honey or margarine directly from its container. This way you don't have to keep stopping to wash up a sticky scale pan or jug. Scales that combine a sensitive measure with a wide-scale range are most useful. I use Avery Health Scales which have a battery and are computerized. You can switch from ounces to grams at the press of a digit, although you only use one measuring system per recipe. The scales also have a timer and they tell you how much fibre, fat or carbohydrate is in the item you are measuring!

SCISSORS *

Kitchen scissors make quick work of cutting and chopping herbs and shaping greaseproof paper for lining dishes. Keeping a pair in the kitchen (hidden from the rest of the family, if necessary) also saves tearing around the house or rummaging in the sewing-box with sticky fingers. Wash and dry them well to prevent rusting.

SIEVE ***

A sieve is essential if you enjoy baking because wholemeal flour benefits by sifting. Introducing air makes a lighter texture and the bran is later returned to the mixture. A sieve can also double as an extra colander. Choose a nylon one if you intend to purée fruit in it.

SPATULA **

There are two types of spatula in my kitchen: a Racle Tout shaped like a little plastic pocket which is firm and ideal for working with dough and other solid mixtures; and a soft, flexible plastic spatula with a long handle which is useful for scraping out the mixing bowl, liquidizer and food processor. The spatulas help make quick work of these jobs.

SPOONS ***

Either the real thing – a tablespoon, dessertspoon and teaspoon – or a spoon measure can be used for measuring during cooking. Using the real thing cuts down on the number of unnecessary kitchen items.

STEAMER **

A stainless steel steamer is invaluable in the vegetarian kitchen because steaming fruit and vegetables prevents the leaching of vitamins and minerals into cooking water which is usually discarded. Steaming also retains flavour and texture – especially of the watery vegetables such as marrows, courgettes and cabbage.

TERRINE/BREAD TIN * *

A glass or ceramic terrine is more versatile than a bread tin because it can be used for making pâté and vegetable terrines, can be put in the microwave oven (which a bread tin can't) and is attractive enough, in some instances, for use at table.

TIMER * *

As one tends to do more than one thing at a time in the kitchen, a timer is invaluable in preventing burnt offerings and lost tempers. You can use your oven timer, a timer on another piece of equipment or the timer on your watch but a simple clockwork timer for particular kitchen use can be easier.

VACUUM FLASK * * *

Choose a wide-mouth 'food' vacuum flask to cut down on the soaking times of dried beans and pulses and to obviate the need to cook dried fruit such as apricots and prunes. These are ready to eat after a soak in boiling water. Pour on the water, seal and leave for a couple of minutes, then drain. This cleans the fruits and removes the oils and preservatives. Cover again and leave. Incidentally, if you do cook dried fruit you need *not* soak it first. You can also make porridge overnight in the flask and take hot food to work in it.

WATER FILTER

If you are not happy with tap water, and bottled water seems expensive, then a water filter is worth considering. Chlorine can affect the taste of tap water, and old pipes can contribute dust, lead or rust. In most filters, activated carbon or charcoal is used to filter the water and remove these substances – most cannot remove fluoride. Unlike water softeners, filters do not remove calcium and magnesium salts, which are protective against heart disease, nor do they add sodium salts. Water filters are sold as jugs, flasks, tap attachments or units that have to be plumbed in.

WOK *

This is not essential but useful if you are keen on stir-frying as it allows the minimum use of oil and distributes heat well. To get the most out of buying a wok, choose a stainless steel version with a steamer tray which fits over the side and a lid. These make it a very versatile piece of equipment.

YOGHURT MAKER *

For a vegetarian, yoghurt can be a staple food and once you get into the habit it's very quick to make your own and save money. My favourite is the Bel Yoghurt Maker. It consists of an insulated flask which contains a one-litre plastic container. There is also a thermometer in the kit to measure the right milk temperature after bringing it to the boil. You put the cooling milk and starter in the container, stand it in the flask, put on the lid and leave it to 'yog'. Afterwards, you lift out the container with its lid and chill it in the fridge. The yoghurt maker is very easy to clean, takes up little space and is far less fussy than electrically operated ones containing individual pots.

MEAL AND MENU PLANNING

There's no doubt that if you plan the week's menu ahead, you will save time. A little advance thought means you don't have to think *each* day about what you are going to eat. Forward planning should mean fewer shopping trips and consequent savings on fares or petrol.

There are a few points to bear in mind. First, try to make your food as varied as possible. By eating a wide range of foods you will increase the different nutrients (vitamins and minerals) in your diet. Extend, if possible, this variety to each day's meals. For example, if you have toast or bread for breakfast, think about something other than sandwiches for lunch – although there is nothing wrong with eating bread again.

Try to have one salad meal a day or, if that's not possible, one meal that includes lightly cooked fresh vegetables. Green leafy vegetables or orange fruit and vegetables are the ones to choose daily for their vitamin A and C and all their other 'goodness'.

The other meal of the day can become the main protein meal, although you will be getting protein in some form or another at most of your meals (see REPLACING MEAT p. 4). Remember you don't need much protein – hardly anyone in Britain goes short of it in their diet.

If necessary, fill up between meals on fresh fruit and vegetable snacks or on wholemeal sandwiches and other low-fat, high-fibre foods.

When planning your meals, try to introduce a few different colours and textures to keep the eye interested and the mouth crunching and chewing and then enjoying softer textures. Varying flavours is important, too. It's boring if you have the same dominant flavour in starter and main course.

Think of each day as a unit in which you want to balance your intake of fat, fibre, sugar and salt. If one meal has quite a bit of fat, then make an effort for the other meals to be low-fat.

Finally, don't worry about having a hot meal each day. A good meal doesn't have to be a hot meal – in fact, the more raw food your diet contains the better. And neither does it matter if you eat your main meal in the evening or in the middle of the day – or even as little snacks throughout the day – as long as the ingredients are healthy and all add up to a good balance.

PART TWO

Recipes for Busy Vegetarian Cooks

QUICK MEALS

To make cooking quicker, you will find what implements you need for making the dishes listed in each recipe under the heading HAVE READY. It's a time-saver if you assemble all these items first and then get cracking.

There are four things *not* listed because you will automatically get these out before you start on virtually all the recipes:

- a sharp vegetable knife
- a chopping-board
- a tablespoon
- a pair of scales.

(There is something else you will always do – even if you're in a hurry, having just flown in from work – and that is wash your hands before you start.)

You will also notice that some recipes have a note about what you can do the previous evening or before going out to work in the morning. This is designed to speed things along, so do check before you decide on a recipe.

However, not everything needs forethought. There are plenty of recipes you can make from standard store-cupboard and fridge/freezer items that will be stocked in a vegetarian kitchen and about which you have read in Part One.

Most of these recipes are meals in themselves, but some have serving suggestions for additional items you might like to serve with the finished dish. For example, you may wish to add a salad – a choice of which you will find on pp. 133–141 – or fresh vegetables, which can be steamed, boiled, baked or cooked in the microwave while you prepare the main course.

And if you don't want to accompany the meal with potatoes or pasta, don't forget about grains or wholemeal bread, served in the continental style without lashings of butter or margarine, but enjoyed in its own right. Bread will go well with most choices (unless it is a component of the main dish) and will fill any gaps in the healthy menu.

NUT RISSOLES

If you have time, brown lentils make tastier rissoles than red ones, but they take thirty minutes or so to cook. However, you may have some already cooked or you could use a can of brown lentils.

MAKES 4 RISSOLES

HAVE READY: saucepan, food processor or grater, frying pan, absorbent kitchen paper.

2oz/50g split red lentils
1 thick slice wholemeal bread
1 onion
4oz/100g mixed nuts (such as cashew pieces and Brazils)

freshly ground black pepper
1 small free-range egg to bind
1 lightly beaten free-range egg
vegetable oil for cooking

Wash and pick over the lentils, then boil for ten minutes until soft. Drain. Make breadcrumbs from the wholemeal slice in a food processor or with a grater. Heat a frying pan and toast the crumbs in it, shaking the pan for even cooking. Sauté the finely diced onion. Finely mill the nuts in the food processor. Mix together the lentils, onion, nuts and the seasoning, binding with a small egg. Dip the rissoles in the beaten egg, roll in breadcrumbs and fry lightly, grill or heat through in the microwave for two minutes or more. Drain on absorbent kitchen paper, if fried.

CARIBBEAN VEGETABLES

SERVES 2

HAVE READY: grater, garlic press, frying pan with lid.

½ red pepper
½ green pepper
2 bell peppers or chillies
1 small sweet potato
1 small plantain
2oz/50g okra

2 cloves garlic
1in/2.5cm piece root ginger
cayenne pepper
pinch cinnamon
2 tbsp vegetable oil

Dice the peppers, bell peppers (or chillies) and the sweet potato.
Slice the plantain and okra.
Crush the garlic and grate the peeled ginger.

Place the vegetables – except the okra and plantain – in a frying pan with the spices and oil.

Sauté for ten minutes.

Stir in the okra, plantain, red and green peppers and cook for fifteen minutes, covered, stirring from time to time to prevent sticking.

Serve with Corn Bread (p. 208).

FROZEN VEGETABLE GRATIN

SERVES 2

HAVE READY: two saucepans, measuring jug, boiling water, food processor or liquidizer, oven-proof serving-dish, grater.

12oz/325g potatoes
1lb/450g vegetable stew pack (or 10oz/275g Sunrise organic pack)
1 vegetable bouillon cube
½pt/300ml boiling water
2 tsp tomato purée
freshly ground black pepper

2 shakes vegetarian Worcestershire sauce
2 tsp arrowroot slaked in water
few tbsp skimmed milk
2oz/50g mature Cheddar cheese, grated

Scrub or peel the potatoes, cut up and boil for about fifteen minutes or until cooked.

Place the stewpack in a saucepan, add the bouillon and the water and cook for about ten minutes (or as instructed on the pack).

When the vegetables are cooked, stir in the tomato purée, pepper and Worcestershire sauce.

Add the arrowroot and stir over the heat until thickened.

Place the vegetables in an oven-proof serving-dish and keep warm.

Drain the potatoes and place in the liquidizer or food processor and blend to a smooth purée with the milk and cheese.

Pile on top of the vegetables and brown quickly under a hot grill.

TORTILLA

SERVES 2

HAVE READY: saucepan, omelette pan, fish-slice, wooden spoon, fork and basin or electric mixer to whisk eggs, grater.

8oz/225g potatoes
½ tbsp olive oil
1 onion, diced
4 free-range eggs

freshly ground black pepper
sea salt
2oz/50g cheese, grated (optional)

Scrub the potatoes and boil for ten to fifteen minutes until almost cooked. Drain and when cool enough to handle cut into small pieces.
Place the oil in the omelette pan and sauté the onion for about five minutes until soft.
Whisk the eggs together with the seasoning.
Add the potatoes to the pan with the onion and cook for a few minutes, turning with a fish-slice or palette knife.
Pour on the frothy eggs and stir round with a wooden spoon until the mixture is almost set.
Flash under a hot grill to cook the top and add the cheese at this stage (if used).
Carefully lift from pan with a fish-slice and serve at once.

SPANISH STYLE

The Spanish often prefer to serve this tortilla cold. It is made without cheese, inverted and left on a plate and when completely cold cut into slices. This is not always to the British taste but is useful if you only want half on one occasion.

WITH TOMATOES

For a change you can add a small can of tomatoes just before adding the eggs to the pan.

EGGS FLORENTINE

SERVES 2

HAVE READY: saucepan, liquidizer or food processor, grater, egg poacher (see recipe below).

11b/450g spinach (or 8oz/225g frozen)

freshly ground black pepper
freshly grated nutmeg

1 tbsp wholemeal flour	2oz/50g Gruyère cheese, grated
1 tbsp vegetable oil	2 free-range eggs
½pt/300ml skimmed milk	a little butter (optional)

Set the oven to 375°F/190°C/Gas 5 – unless using the quicker version below.

Wash the spinach and cook in a large saucepan without the addition of further water.

Transfer to a liquidizer or food processor with the remaining ingredients, except the eggs and butter, if used.

Blend to a sauce and return to a clean pan and stir over a moderate heat until the mixture thickens. Place in a gratin dish or similar ovenproof dish and make two wells to take the eggs.

Break the eggs into the wells carefully and put a little pepper and a dot of butter (if used) on top.

Place in the oven and cook for ten minutes to poach the eggs.

Serve with warm wholemeal bread or rolls.

QUICKER STILL. . .

If you like, you can poach the eggs in an egg poacher or boiling water while the spinach is cooking and then just top the mixture with the eggs.

EASY-PEASY TACO DINNER

SERVES 2

HAVE READY: saucepan, grater.

15oz/425g can Batchelors Chili Beans	OPTIONAL:
6 taco or tortilla shells*	2oz/50g Cheddar cheese, grated
	¼ lettuce, shredded

Heat the beans in a saucepan or in the microwave.

Warm the taco shells under a grill, in the conventional oven or microwave.

Stuff the shells with the beans and top – if you feel up to it – with grated cheese and shredded lettuce.

QUICK BEAN TACOS

SERVES 2

HAVE READY: saucepan, grater.

1 onion
4 tomatoes
14oz/400g can brown beans
2in/5cm piece cucumber

6 taco or tortilla shells*
¼ lettuce, shredded
3oz/75g mature Cheddar, grated

Dice the onion and chop the tomatoes and place in a saucepan with the beans.

Heat for about fifteen minutes, then stir in the diced cucumber.

Warm the taco shells under a grill, in the conventional oven or microwave.

Spoon the mixture into the shells and top with lettuce and cheese.

TACO DINNER

SERVES 2

HAVE READY: saucepan, grater.

4oz/100g mushrooms
1 onion, diced
½ red pepper, diced
½ tbsp vegetable oil
⅛pt/75ml water

sachet taco seasoning mix
6 taco or tortilla shells*
¼ lettuce
1 large tomato
2oz/50g red Leicester cheese, grated

Place the mushrooms, diced onion and pepper in a saucepan with the oil and cook over a moderate heat for ten minutes until softened. Add the water and the sachet of taco seasoning mix, stir well and continue cooking for another three or four minutes.

Warm the taco shells under a grill, in the conventional oven or microwave.

Wash and shred the lettuce and slice the tomato.

Place the mushroom mixture in the taco shells and garnish with the lettuce, tomato and grated cheese.

The Mexican custom is to put the cheese and lettuce in the taco shell on top of the hot filling.

*BUYING TACOS

I think the best readily available taco shells are from Casa Fiesta, sold in supermarkets and health-food shops. The seasoning mix comes in the box with twelve taco shells.

CHILLI AND PITTAS

SERVES 2

HAVE READY: saucepan, can-opener, wooden spoon.

3 green chillies
2 cloves garlic
1 large onion
1 green pepper
1 tbsp vegetable oil
1 tsp ground cumin

7oz/200g can tomatoes
14oz/400g can red kidney beans
4 large, oval wholemeal pitta
    breads (or 4–6 smaller, round
    ones)

Dice the chillies, garlic, onion and pepper and place in a saucepan with the oil and cumin and sauté for ten minutes.
Add the tomatoes and break them up with the back of a wooden spoon. Cook for a further five minutes, uncovered.
Add the beans and heat through for five minutes.
Warm the bread under a grill, in the conventional oven or microwave, but do not let it crisp or become fragile because you are going to stuff it with the chilli filling.
Fill the warmed bread with the chilli mixture and serve at once.

POTATO CRISP GRATIN

If you don't have time to cook potatoes, or if you're just a crisp freak, try this one.

SERVES 2

HAVE READY: steamer to fit inside the saucepan, second saucepan, wooden spoon, gratin dish, grater.

8oz/225g broccoli
1 tbsp wholemeal flour
1 tbsp vegetable oil
⅓pt/200ml skimmed milk
1 tsp meaux mustard

freshly ground black pepper
3oz/75g Cheddar cheese, grated
1 small packet plain potato crisps,
   unsalted

Steam the broccoli for about eight minutes until tender but still with some 'bite'.

Stir together the flour and oil in a saucepan over a moderate heat to make a roux.

Gradually stir in the milk, cooking a little between additions. Alternatively, make in the microwave by cooking the flour and oil in a jug on HIGH for one minute, stirring halfway through, then adding the milk and cooking for thirty-second periods, stirring after each, until thickened.

Stir in the mustard, pepper and half the cheese.

Place the broccoli in the bottom of a gratin or other oven-proof shallow dish.

Top with the cheese sauce.

Break up the crisps slightly and mix with the cheese, then toss over the top of the dish.

Place under a hot grill for a few minutes or in the microwave on HIGH for a minute or two.

Serve with grilled tomatoes, cut in half with cut-side uppermost to grill and sprinkled with black pepper. Or bake them in the microwave.

VEGETABLES WITH CORIANDER

SERVES 2

HAVE READY: food flask or Thermos, two saucepans, garlic press.

NIGHT BEFORE/MORNING: Soak the lentils in boiling water in a food flask or Thermos to reduce cooking time.

4oz/100g brown lentils
1 bay leaf
1 clove garlic
1 large onion
1 tbsp vegetable oil

1 tbsp white mustard seed
1 tsp ground coriander
6oz/175g sweet potato
2 ripe tomatoes
1 tbsp freshly chopped coriander

Boil the soaked lentils in twice their volume of water for twenty to thirty minutes with the bay leaf. Crush the garlic and dice the onion. Place in a saucepan with the oil, mustard seed and ground coriander and sauté for five minutes until soft and transparent.

Add the diced sweet potato and the chopped tomatoes and mix well. Cover and cook in their own steam, stirring frequently for fifteen minutes. Drain the cooked lentils and stir into the vegetables. Finally mix in the freshly chopped coriander.

TOFU AND CORN BURGERS

SERVES 2

HAVE READY: mixing bowl, fork, pastry board, frying pan, grater, fish-slice, absorbent kitchen paper.

10oz/275g tofu
4oz/100g onion, grated
4oz/100g sweetcorn
sea salt
freshly ground black pepper

2oz/50g wholemeal breadcrumbs
2 tbsp freshly chopped parsley
1 tbsp wholemeal flour (for board)
vegetable oil for frying

Place the tofu in a bowl and mash to a purée with a fork.
Stir in the grated onion and the rest of the ingredients.
Form into burger shapes on a lightly floured board.
Fry in a little vegetable oil and drain on absorbent kitchen paper before serving.
You can also grill the burgers or heat them in a microwave on HIGH for two minutes each side.

TOMATO AND COURGETTE GRATIN

SERVES 2

HAVE READY: grater, saucepan, gratin dish.

8oz/225g courgettes
8oz/225g tomatoes
1 tbsp vegetable oil
freshly ground black pepper

1 tsp finely chopped thyme
2 thick slices wholemeal bread
2oz/50g Gruyère cheese

Slice the courgettes and tomatoes and place in a heavy-based sauce-pan with the oil. Cover and cook in their own steam for fifteen minutes, adding the pepper and thyme after about five minutes. Stir occasionally.

Grate the bread and the cheese, then toss together.

Place the cooked tomatoes and courgettes in a dish and top with the breadcrumb and cheese mixture. Place under a hot grill for about seven minutes, being careful not to let it burn.

TOMATO SCOTCH EGGS

SERVES 2

HAVE READY: baking tray, grater, egg-boiling pan, teaspoon, mixing bowl.

2 free-range eggs
4oz/100g wholemeal breadcrumbs
2oz/50g mixed groundnuts
1 tomato

4oz/100g onion, grated
1 tsp tomato purée
1 tsp dried herbs of choice

Set the oven to 400°F/200°C/Gas 6.

Boil the eggs for about seven to ten minutes until they are hard-boiled. Plunge into cold water and when cool enough to handle, shell them.

Mix together the crumbs and nuts, chopped tomato, grated onion and tomato purée with the herbs. If necessary, bind with a little ketchup to make a soft paste.

Form the paste around the eggs and place them on a baking sheet.

Bake for ten minutes each side.

Serve hot or cold.

CAULIFLOWER GRATIN

SERVES 2

HAVE READY: heavy-based saucepans, wooden spoon, grater, oven-proof serving-dish, garlic press.

1 onion
1 clove garlic

1 small cauliflower
1 tbsp wholemeal flour

1 tbsp vegetable oil or soft
  vegetable margarine
½pt/300ml skimmed milk
freshly ground black pepper
1 tsp mustard powder

2oz/50g mature Cheddar cheese,
  grated
1oz/25g mature Cheddar cheese,
  grated

Dice the onion and crush the garlic.

Place in a heavy-based pan with a well-fitting lid. Sauté in a little oil for five minutes, stirring from time to time.

Break the cauliflower into florets and add to the pan. Continue cooking with the lid on, so the vegetables cook partially in their own steam while you make the sauce.

Place the flour and oil in a saucepan and stir over a moderate heat to make a roux. Gradually stir in the milk, cooking between additions. Remove from the heat and stir in the pepper, mustard and the larger amount of cheese.

Place the cauliflower in the bottom of an oven-proof serving-dish and top with the sauce. Sprinkle the rest of the cheese over the gratin and put under a hot grill until it melts and is golden brown.

FRESH TOMATO FLAN

SERVES 4

HAVE READY: a rolling pin, pastry board, 8in/20cm flan ring and baking tray, greaseproof paper, baking beans, wire cooling-tray, large basin, screw-top jar.

NIGHT BEFORE/MORNING: Remove the pastry (or quiche pastry case) from the freezer to thaw. Or buy a fresh pastry case on the day.

1 packet wholemeal shortcrust
  pastry (or pastry case)
2lb/900g fresh ripe tomatoes
4 tbsp olive oil
juice of half an orange

2 tbsp freshly chopped chives
freshly ground black pepper
1 tbsp wholemeal flour (for board)
grated orange rind for garnish

Set the oven to 400°F/200°C/Gas 6

Roll out the pastry and line an 8in/20cm flan ring. Line with greaseproof paper and fill with baking beans. Bake blind for fifteen minutes. Remove the paper and beans and return to the oven for a further five minutes. Remove and cool on a wire cooling tray. (Easier still, use a thawed quiche pastry case or a freshly bought one.)

Plunge the tomatoes into boiling water for two minutes, then remove and place in cold water. This should make it easy to skin them. After skinning, slice in rings. Mix together the rest of the ingredients in a clean screw-top jar and shake vigorously. Arrange the tomatoes in the base of the pastry case and spoon the dressing over the top. Garnish with a little orange rind and serve at once.

LENTIL PATTIES

MAKES 8 PATTIES

HAVE READY: saucepan, pastry board, frying pan, absorbent kitchen paper, food processor.

3oz/75g split red lentils
4oz/100g cottage cheese
2oz/50g fine oatmeal
1 tsp ground cumin

1 tsp ground coriander
1 tbsp wholemeal flour (for board)
vegetable oil

Boil the lentils in plenty of water for about ten to fifteen minutes until cooked.
Drain.
Put them in a food processor and add the rest of the ingredients.
Form into patties on a lightly floured board and then fry lightly in a little vegetable oil. Drain on absorbent kitchen paper.

Serve with a salad and/or potatoes.

TABBOULEH

Deliciously minty, cracked wheat salad

SERVES 4

HAVE READY: saucepan or large basin, lemon squeezer.

4oz/100g cracked wheat/bulgur
½ cucumber
1 green pepper
4 spring onions or

½ onion
2 tbsp freshly chopped mint
juice of half a lemon
freshly ground black pepper

Either boil the cracked wheat/bulgur for ten minutes in twice its volume of water or leave it to stand for fifteen minutes until the grain has swelled and softened.

Drain and squeeze dry, if necessary.

Dice the cucumber, pepper and onion. Mix them in with the cracked wheat, together with the rest of the ingredients – the mint, lemon and pepper. Refrigerate before eating.

FALAFEL BURGERS

Tasty egg-sized savouries, although you could make them into larger burger sizes for a main meal.

MAKES 14 EGG-SIZED 'BURGERS'

HAVE READY: egg-boiling saucepan, liquidizer or food processor, can-opener.

2 free-range eggs	1 tbsp vegetable oil
1 red pepper	10oz/275g can chickpeas
1 clove garlic	1 tbsp freshly chopped parsley
1 onion	freshly ground black pepper

Boil the eggs for about seven minutes until hard. Dice the pepper, garlic and onion and sauté in the oil until soft and just cooked but not browned. This takes about ten minutes.

Remove from heat and place in liquidizer or food processor with the drained chickpeas and process to a purée.

Remove and place in a bowl. Stir in the parsley and pepper.

Finely dice the eggs and stir in. Mould into egg-size shapes or burger-size pieces. Serve cold or just warm.

SPICY RICE

SERVES 2

HAVE READY: deep heavy-based saucepan or wok, wooden spoon or spatula, saucepan for cooking rice, two small serving-dishes.

4oz/100g brown rice
1in/2.5cm root ginger, grated
1 clove garlic, crushed
2 tbsp vegetable oil

4oz/100g baby sweetcorn
4oz/100g mange tout peas
sea salt
freshly ground black pepper

SPEEDY TIPS: Add the rice to boiling water and cook that first, then prepare and cook the rest of the dish.

Wash the rice and boil in plenty of water. Place the ginger and garlic in the oil in a heavy-based pan and stir over a low heat for five minutes.
Add the corn and mange tout peas and continue to stir-fry over a moderate heat for another five minutes.
Place the rice on serving-dishes and top with the vegetable mixture.

AUBERGINE ESPAGNOL

SERVES 2

HAVE READY: heavy-based saucepan with well-fitting lid.

Boil some rice or potatoes if you would like them with this dish.

1 large Spanish onion, diced
12oz/325g aubergine, cubed
2 tbsp vegetable oil
8oz/225g tomatoes, cubed

14oz/400g can red kidney beans
¼pt/150ml vegetable stock
1 tbsp sliced green olives

Place the onion and aubergine in a deep saucepan with the oil and stir well over the heat for five minutes.
Add the tomatoes and continue cooking for ten minutes.
Stir in the beans and the stock and continue cooking, covered, for another ten minutes.
Stir in the olives and heat through.

Serve with plain brown rice or potatoes.

BROAD BEAN RISOTTO

SERVES 2

HAVE READY: food flask or Thermos, garlic press, two saucepans, measuring jug.

NIGHT BEFORE/MORNING: Soak the rice in a food flask or Thermos in enough boiling water to cover to one inch over the top of the rice.

4oz/100g brown rice
¾pt/450ml vegetable stock
1lb/450g broad beans, unshelled
1 clove garlic, crushed

1 tbsp vegetable oil
1 tbsp turmeric
1 tbsp freshly chopped basil

Place the soaked rice in a saucepan and boil with the stock while you shell the beans.

Place the garlic in a saucepan with the oil and turmeric and stir for about three minutes over a low heat to soften. Add the beans and stir in. Then transfer the rice and stock to the pan and stir well. Once combined, leave to finish cooking for about twenty minutes until the rest of the liquid is absorbed and the rice and beans are cooked. Sprinkle with basil.

LENTIL AND SPINACH FILO

SERVES 2

HAVE READY: baking sheet, saucepan, pastry brush.

4oz/100g split red lentils
4oz/100g frozen spinach (or
    8oz/225g fresh, washed spinach)

2 tsp ground cumin
6 sheets filo pastry, unfrozen
skimmed milk for glazing

Set the oven to 400°F/200°C/Gas 6.

Cook the lentils in plenty of boiling water for ten minutes, then drain. Thaw the spinach in a saucepan over a low heat or in a microwave. (Or cook the washed fresh spinach without the addition of any more water.) Then stir in the lentils and the cumin and, if liked, liquidize to a smooth consistency – or leave as it is.

Place the sheets of pastry on a baking sheet and pile the lentil mixture down the centre, lengthways. Fold in the two ends and then roll up as you would a Swiss Roll. Brush the top with milk and roll over on to the other side. Glaze with milk and bake for fifteen minutes.

Note

There are about 20–24 sheets of filo pastry in a box. It is sold frozen.

RICOTTA FILO

SERVES 2–3

HAVE READY: baking sheet, liquidizer or food processor, pastry brush, saucepan, serving-dish.

8 sheets filo pastry
4oz/100g frozen spinach (or
    8oz/225g fresh, washed spinach)
4oz/100g ricotta cheese

1 tbsp freshly chopped parsley
freshly ground black pepper
oil to glaze pastry

Set the oven to 400°F/200°C/Gas 6.

Lightly oil the filo pastry in two lots of four sheets on a baking sheet and bake for ten minutes until crispy and golden.

Thaw the frozen spinach in a saucepan over a low heat or in a microwave. (Or cook the fresh, washed spinach without the addition of any more water.) Liquidize the spinach with the cheese, parsley and pepper.

Remove the pastry from the oven. Place one, four-sheet layer on a serving-dish, cover with the filling and top with the second layer. Serve at once.

SIX-GRAIN PAELLA

SERVES 2

HAVE READY: saucepan, paella pan.

4oz/100g Jordans Country Rice
    and Grains
1 green pepper
1 leek
2 courgettes

1 onion
2 cloves garlic
1 tbsp olive oil
½pt/300ml vegetable stock
8oz/225g smoked tofu

Put the grains on to boil for about fifteen to twenty minutes while you prepare the vegetables.

Slice the pepper into rings and dice the leek. Slice the courgettes. Dice the onion and crush the garlic.

Add the garlic and onion to the paella pan with the oil and cook over a moderate heat to soften. Add the other vegetables and sauté for five minutes. Drain the grains and toss into the pan, stir well and then pour over the stock and continue cooking at a light boil for fifteen minutes until the grains are soft.

Dice the tofu and press lightly into the paella for the last ten minutes of cooking but do not stir again.

Note

Jordans Country Rice and Grains is a mixture of brown rice, whole oats, barley, wheat, rye, buckwheat and sesame seeds.

SPINACH SOUFFLÉS

MAKES 4 SOUFFLÉS

HAVE READY: saucepan, electric mixer fitted with whisk attachment, four ramekins or soufflé dishes, pastry brush, wooden spoon.

NIGHT BEFORE/MORNING: Put the frozen spinach out to thaw.

4oz/100g frozen spinach (or
  8oz/225g fresh, washed spinach)
1 tbsp vegetable oil
1 tbsp wholemeal flour
½pt/300ml skimmed milk

2 free-range egg yolks
freshly ground black pepper
2oz/50g Gruyère cheese, grated
3 free-range egg-whites

Set the oven to 375°F/190°C/Gas 5.

Lightly oil the four ramekins or soufflé dishes.

Thaw the spinach in a saucepan over a low heat or in a microwave. (Or cook the fresh, washed spinach without the addition of any more water.) Chop it finely.

Place the oil and flour in a saucepan and stir over a moderate heat to make a roux.

Gradually add the milk, stirring all the time until the sauce thickens. Alternatively make the roux in a microwave by mixing the oil and flour and cooking on MEDIUM for one minute, stirring halfway through. Remove and add the milk, then cook for thirty-second periods on HIGH, stirring after each one until the sauce thickens. Stir in the chopped spinach.

Remove from the heat and stir in the egg yolks, pepper and cheese.

Whisk the whites until stiff and then fold in, using a metal table-spoon.
Pour into the prepared dishes and bake for twenty minutes.
Serve at once.

INDIAN VEGETARIAN

SERVES 2

HAVE READY: large saucepan for the rice, heavy-based sauce-pan with well-fitting lid for the vegetables, garlic press, can-opener.

4oz/100g brown rice
1 clove garlic
1 onion
1 tbsp vegetable oil
2 large potatoes
1 aubergine

1 green pepper
1 tsp each cumin and coriander
¼ tsp red chilli powder
1 tsp Rechard marinating paste
14oz/400g can tomatoes

Boil the rice in plenty of water for thirty minutes while you prepare the vegetables.
Crush the garlic and dice the onion and place in a heavy-based saucepan with a well-fitting lid and cook in the oil over a moderate heat for five minutes. Scrub and dice the potatoes, dice the aubergine and slice the pepper. Add these to the pan. Stir well, adding the spices and paste, cover and continue cooking for ten minutes.
Add the tomatoes and break them up with the back of a wooden spoon. Mix in well and cover. Finish cooking for ten minutes until the rice is ready.

ONION TART

SERVES 2

HAVE READY: saucepan, flan ring and baking tray, rolling pin, mixing bowl.

NIGHT BEFORE/MORNING: defrost the packet of pastry.

1 packet frozen wholemeal pastry
2 onions
½ tbsp vegetable oil
freshly ground black pepper

8oz/225g Quark
2 free-range eggs
4oz/100g strained Greek yoghurt
2oz/50g Gruyère cheese

114

Set the oven to 400°F/200°C/Gas 6.

Roll out the pastry and line an 8in/20cm flan ring on a baking tray.
Dice the onions and soften in the oil over a moderate heat. Season
and remove from the heat.
Beat together the Quark, eggs and yoghurt.
Grate the cheese.
Mix together all the ingredients and fill the pastry case.
Bake for thirty minutes.

EGGS EN PIPERADE

SERVES 2

HAVE READY: heavy-based pan that can be used on the hob
and then transferred to the oven, garlic press, wooden spoon.

1 red pepper	sea salt
1 green pepper	freshly ground pepper
1 onion	2 drops Tabasco
2 cloves garlic	3 ripe tomatoes
1 tbsp vegetable oil	2 free-range eggs

Set the oven to 375°F/190°C/Gas 5.

Finely dice the peppers, onion and garlic and sauté in the oil in a
covered pan for five minutes until soft.
Add the seasoning and the roughly chopped tomatoes and continue
cooking for fifteen minutes in the covered pan.
Make two wells in the mixture and carefully break one egg into each.
Transfer the pan to the oven and bake for ten minutes for a set egg
(slightly less for a softer egg).

CHEESE WHEAT SLICE

SERVES 2

HAVE READY: oven-proof dish or 6in/15cm tin, grater, bowl.

4oz/100g cracked wheat/bulgur	3oz/75g Cheddar cheese
2oz/50g wholemeal breadcrumbs	1 free-range egg
1 large onion	2 tsp mustard

Set the oven to 400°F/200°C/Gas 6.

Pour enough boiling water on the cracked wheat to almost cover and leave to stand while you prepare the other ingredients.
Place the breadcrumbs in a bowl and grate in the onion and cheese. Beat in the egg and mustard.
Place in a lightly oiled dish or tin and bake for twenty minutes.

Slice and serve with salad.

MINI NUT-ROASTS

MAKES 4 MINI-LOAVES

HAVE READY: four mini-loaf tins, food processor to grind the nuts, grater, wooden spoon.

4oz/100g mixed nuts	1 green pepper
2oz/50g wholemeal breadcrumbs	⅛pt/75ml water
1 onion	1 tbsp tomato purée

Set the oven to 400°F/200°C/Gas 6.

Grind the nuts in a food processor and stir in the breadcrumbs.
Grate the onion and dice the pepper and add to the nut mixture. Mix to a paste with the water and tomato purée.
Fill the tins, smooth the tops and then bake for twenty-five minutes.

Serve with fresh vegetables.

PRESTO PIZZA

SERVES 2

HAVE READY: two baking trays, cheese-slicer, grater.

NIGHT BEFORE/MORNING: defrost pizza bases, if necessary.

2 wholemeal pizza bases	3 sticks celery
2 tbsp tomato purée	1 red pepper
1 pinch dried basil	2oz/50g pine kernels
3 tomatoes	2oz/50g black olives
2 carrots	6oz/175g Mozarella cheese

Set the oven to 400°F/200°C/Gas 6.

Place the pizza bases on baking trays, spread with the purée and then sprinkle over the basil. Chop the tomatoes and place in a saucepan with the grated carrots and sliced celery and pepper. Cover and cook in the vegetables' own steam for ten minutes. Spread the mixture over the top of the pizzas and sprinkle the pine kernels over the top. Then arrange the olives.

Cover with thin slices of the cheese and bake for twenty minutes.

Note

For a *really* quick pizza, cover the base with the purée (as above), top with sliced tomato and avocado plus the cheese and bake for twenty minutes.

If you want to make your own bases you can, if you work quickly, still have the pizza on the table in forty-five minutes (see recipe in 'Cooking Ahead' p. 211).

MUSHROOM GRATIN

SERVES 2

HAVE READY: a saucepan, oven-proof dish, grater.

4oz/100g split red lentils	2oz/50g wholemeal breadcrumbs
1 onion	1oz/25g Cheddar cheese, grated
4oz/100g mushrooms	

Boil the lentils in plenty of water for ten minutes.

Dice the onion and slice the mushrooms. Cook in their own steam in a covered pan for ten minutes (or microwave on HIGH for three minutes.

Mix the breadcrumbs and the cheese.

Place the lentils in the bottom of the dish and then add the mushrooms. Sprinkle the breadcrumbs over the top and bake for fifteen minutes.

LIGHT SNACKS AND SALADS

It is not every day that you come home ravenously hungry, yet it is still nice to enjoy an evening meal at home, especially if shared with a partner, family or flatmates. If you have endured a business lunch, you may only want a light supper and while the following recipes require some preparation (so you feel you have completed the 'ritual' of preparing something to eat), they are not substantial or difficult meals.

When you don't want to prepare hot meals, a salad is an excellent alternative, especially if you have not had any other raw food during the day. Salads are refreshing, light and relatively quick and easy to prepare.

SNACKS

POTATO CAKES

MAKES 6 CAKES

HAVE READY: Two saucepans, frying pan, absorbent kitchen paper, food processor or liquidizer or potato masher, colander, pastry board.

1lb/450g potatoes
4 tbsp skimmed milk
1 large onion
1 clove garlic
1 tbsp olive oil
1 tsp ground cumin

1 tsp ground coriander
¼ tsp chilli powder
4oz/100g peas
1 tbsp wholemeal flour (for board)
vegetable oil for frying

Scrub and boil the potatoes in plenty of water (first cutting them into smaller pieces will speed the cooking). Drain and place in a food processor or liquidizer with the milk and blend to a soft purée (or simply mash them).

Dice the onion and garlic and sauté in the oil with the spices over a moderate heat so that the vegetables soften but do not brown.

Cook the peas and drain.

Stir the peas and the onion mixture into the potato and form into cakes on a lightly floured board.

Fry in a little vegetable oil and drain on a piece of absorbent kitchen paper before serving.

CORN-CAKE FRITTERS

MAKES 10 FRITTERS

HAVE READY: mixing bowl, sieve, frying pan, fish-slice or palette knife, absorbent kitchen paper.

4oz/100g wholemeal flour	4oz/100g sweetcorn kernels
1 free-range egg	sea salt
¼pt/150ml skimmed milk	freshly ground black pepper
2oz/50g cheese of choice, grated	vegetable oil for frying

Sift the flour into a mixing bowl, adding the bran left in the sieve.

Break the egg into a well in the flour and add a little milk. Whisk lightly with a fork to work the liquid into the flour, gradually adding more milk as you progress.

Stir in the grated cheese, sweetcorn kernels and then season to taste.

Heat a little vegetable oil in a frying pan and when hot, but not smoking, add a couple of tablespoonfuls of the mixture at a time.

Cook the fritters, turning with a fish-slice or palette knife, until both sides are golden brown.

Drain on kitchen paper briefly to remove excess oil.

CHEESE AND FRUIT PLATTER

A delicious mixture of fruit and cheese for a lunch or supper – or even a late breakfast. Choose from the lower fat cheeses such as:

119

- cottage, ricotta, lebne
- Brie, Camembert
- Edam, Gouda
- or fat-reduced hard cheeses.

If you do not like fat-reduced hard cheese, have a small portion of standard mature Cheddar or similar (grating makes it go further) and a large amount of cottage cheese. The suggestion below uses tropical fruits but you can equally well use everyday fruits or combine fresh and dried fruits.

SERVES 2

1 mango	individual portions of Camembert
1 pawpaw or papaya	(or cheese of choice)
½ melon	½ small tub of cottage cheese

Peel and slice the fruits.
Arrange slices of fruit with the cheeses on a serving plate.

Serve with wholemeal crispbread, biscuits or crackers, if liked.

BAGNA CAUDA

SERVES 2–4

This is an Italian dip traditionally made with olive oil, double cream, anchovies and walnuts. It is deliciously creamy and very high in calories. This version is a vegetable-based one that is very tasty but has far fewer calories. It can be served in the ceramic *bagna cauda* dish that has a glazed bowl set over a night-light to keep it warm.

HAVE READY: saucepan, liquidizer, *bagna cauda* dish, garlic press.

12oz/325g sweet potato	⅛pt/75ml skimmed milk
3 cloves garlic	1 ¼pt/150ml single cream
½ tbsp vegetable oil	

Scrub the potato and chop it up. Boil in a saucepan (or cook on HIGH in the microwave) until soft – about ten to fifteen minutes depending on the size of the pieces. Drain and place in a liquidizer.

Crush the garlic and sauté in the oil until soft.

Add to the liquidizer with the milk and cream. Blend to a creamy purée.

Place in a *bagna cauda* dish and serve with crudités, toast or crispbread.

LENTIL PÂTÉ

SERVES 2

Use with crudités or spread on hot toast, Crisp Rolls or crispbread.

HAVE READY: two ramekins, two saucepans (one for the lentils and one for the vegetables), liquidizer or food processor.

4oz/100g split red lentils	2 cloves garlic, crushed
3 bay leaves	½ tbsp vegetable oil
1 small onion, diced	freshly ground black pepper
½ red or green pepper, diced	

Wash the lentils and cook in boiling water with the bay leaves for ten to fifteen minutes until they have absorbed the water and are soft. Drain, if necessary, and remove bay leaves.

Gently cook the onion, pepper and garlic in a saucepan in the oil, stirring for five minutes until softened.

Place the cooked lentils and vegetables in a liquidizer or food processor and blend to a purée. Season with pepper.

Put the mixture in two ramekins and cool quickly by placing in the freezer for ten minutes.

QUICK STUFFED PEPPER

SERVES 2

HAVE READY: saucepan (or microwave dish with lid), second saucepan (if not microwaving), can-opener, serving-dish.

2 green peppers (or red, if you
   prefer)

1 can Whole Earth Brown Rice and
   Vegetables
freshly ground black pepper

Halve and deseed the peppers and boil for ten minutes (or microwave, covered, on HIGH with 4 tbsp water for four minutes).
While the peppers are cooking, heat the rice for one minute, as
directed on the can.
Drain the peppers, place on the serving-dish and spoon the rice into
them.
Voilà!

SIMPLE 'SOUFFLÉ'

SERVES 2

HAVE READY: liquidizer, soufflé dish.

½pt/300ml skimmed milk
3 free-range eggs

7oz/200g can sweetcorn kernels
freshly ground black pepper

Set the oven to 400°F/200°C/Gas 6.

Pour the milk into a liquidizer and add the eggs.
Blend until frothy.
Place the sweetcorn in a small soufflé dish and season with pepper.
Pour the egg mixture on top and bake for twenty minutes.

Serve with a salad.

BLUE CHEESE TOASTY

SERVES 1

HAVE READY: toasted sandwich maker.

½ bunch watercress
4 slices wholemeal bread

1oz/25g blue cheese
no-added-sugar chutney (optional)

Wash and trim the watercress, if necessary.
Place two slices of bread in the toaster and put the cheese and

watercress on top. Cover with the other slices of bread and toast according to the directions on your machine.

Serve with chutney, if liked.

Note

You do not need to spread the bread with butter or margarine either inside or out. The sandwich will be crispy on the outside without any fat and moist inside due to the release of moisture during the cooking process.

If you do not have a toasted sandwich maker, make the sandwiches in the usual way, halve them and toast both sides under a conventional grill.

DIPS FOR GLOBE ARTICHOKES

These dips are each enough for two people.

HAVE READY: kitchen scissors, basin, saucepan (or large soufflé microwave oven-proof dish), boiling water, fork.

To prepare the artichokes, wash them well, trim off the tops of the leaves with scissors, and boil them in plenty of water. This will take twenty to forty minutes, depending on whether the artichokes are small and young or older and bigger. (Or you can cook them in a microwave. Place in a deep soufflé dish and fill two thirds with boiling water. Cook on HIGH for ten minutes.)

MAYONNAISE-STYLE DIP

1 tbsp mayonnaise
1 tbsp Quark or other low-fat, soft white cheese

juice of half a lemon
1 tbsp freshly chopped chives

Simply mix all the ingredients together and place in an attractive small bowl.

RASPBERRY VINAIGRETTE

4 tbsp olive oil
1½ tbsp raspberry vinegar

freshly ground black pepper
2 tsp meaux mustard

Place all the ingredients in a clean screw-top jar and shake vigorously. Then pour into a pretty serving-bowl.

BLUE CHEESE DIP

1oz/25g blue cheese
3 tbsp skimmed milk
1 tbsp cream, single or double

Mash the cheese in the milk and cream. Serve in a bowl. (If you want a really creamy dip, use a liquidizer that can cope with small amounts.)

COUSCOUS PATTIES WITH SAUCE

MAKES 8 PATTIES

HAVE READY: basin, two saucepans, grater.

4oz/100g couscous
1 onion
1 green chilli
1 clove garlic
1in/2.5cm root ginger
1 tbsp olive oil
1 tbsp shoyu sauce
1 tbsp lemon juice
2 tbsp fine oatmeal

SAUCE
3 tbsp shoyu sauce
1 tbsp brown rice vinegar
3 tbsp orange juice
1 dsp tomato purée
1 dsp Demerara sugar
2 tsp arrowroot slaked in water

Boil the couscous in plenty of water for ten minutes.
Finely dice the onion and chilli, crush the garlic, grate the ginger and place all in a saucepan with the oil and sauté for five minutes until softened.
Drain the couscous and mix all the ingredients, including the shoyu sauce and lemon juice, together.
Then form into patties and roll in the oatmeal.
Grill each side for seven minutes.
To make the sauce, combine all the listed ingredients and stir in a saucepan over a moderate heat until the sugar has dissolved and the sauce has thickened.

HOMEMADE HUMMUS

SERVES 4
(but will store for a week or so in the fridge)

HAVE READY: food processor or liquidizer, garlic press, lemon squeezer, two serving-dishes.

10oz/275g can chickpeas
4oz/100g tahini (sesame seed spread)
juice of 2–3 lemons
freshly ground black pepper

4oz/100g Quark
1 tsp ground cumin
2 cloves garlic, crushed
freshly chopped parsley

Drain the chickpeas and place in a food processor or liquidizer with the rest of the ingredients.

Blend to a fine purée and place in one or two serving dishes, depending on how much you are going to use initially. Decorate the top by making swirls with a fork and sprinkle with finely chopped parsley.

CONTINENTAL LENTILS

SERVES 2

HAVE READY: saucepan, serving-dish.

NIGHT BEFORE/MORNING: Pick over the lentils to remove grit and stones.

4oz/100g whole green lentils, soaked
2 bay leaves
2 tbsp olive oil

1 tbsp wine vinegar
2 cloves garlic, crushed
1 tsp meaux mustard

Rinse the lentils and boil in plenty of water with the bay leaves for about twenty-five to thirty minutes.

Mix together the remaining ingredients and toss the hot lentils in them.

Arrange on a serving-dish.

Serve with wholemeal bread or rolls and a salad.

MARINATED MUSHROOMS

SERVES 2

HAVE READY: saucepan, measuring jug, basin, individual serving-bowls, garlic press.

NIGHT BEFORE/MORNING: If you have time, it's a quick dish to make for the evening or for next day's lunchbox or supper.

1 clove garlic	4 tbsp white wine vinegar
1 stick celery	¼pt/150ml dry white wine
1 carrot	1 bay leaf
2 shallots	4 peppercorns
½ red pepper	8oz/225g button mushrooms

Finely chop the garlic, celery, carrot, shallots and pepper and add to the vinegar, wine and remaining ingredients – except the mushrooms.

Place in a saucepan, cover and cook over a moderate heat for ten minutes.

Add the mushrooms (which have been wiped clean) and cook over a low heat for a further ten minutes.

Transfer to a basin and allow to cool.

Then leave to stand overnight or for the day.

Serve in bowls with toast, crackers or pitta bread.

BROWN BEAN PÂTÉ

SERVES 2

HAVE READY: can-opener, grater, lemon squeezer, food processor or liquidizer, serving-dish.

14oz/400g can brown beans	1 tbsp olive oil
1 large onion	4 tbsp natural yoghurt (strained) or
sea salt	low fat cheese
juice of half a lemon	freshly ground black pepper

Drain the beans and place in a liquidizer or food processor.

Grate the onion over a bowl to collect the juice.

Add the juice and the rest of the ingredients to the food processor and blend to the required consistency for your pâté.
Arrange on the serving-dish.

Serve with hot bread or toast, pitta bread, salad or crudités.

CHICKPEAS WITH POMEGRANATES

SERVES 2

HAVE READY: fruit squeezer, saucepan, can-opener, garlic press.

1 onion	2 pomegranates
2 cloves garlic	¼ tsp chilli powder
½ tbsp vegetable oil	1 large (8oz/225g) potato
2 tsp garam masala	14oz/400g can chickpeas

Dice the onion and crush the garlic.
Cook in a saucepan with the oil and the garam masala for five minutes or until the vegetables soften.
Squeeze the juice from the pomegranates and add to the mixture with the chilli powder.
Cube the potato and add. Cover and continue cooking for ten minutes, stirring from time to time to prevent the potato sticking to the pan.
Drain the chickpeas and put them in. Cover and cook for a further five minutes until heated through.

Serve with Indian bread, if available, or pitta bread or rice.

REALLY CHEESEY PÂTÉ

Eat this with Crisp Rolls, crackers, crispbread, toast or crudités for a light supper. It is also good with slices of fruit, such as pears and apples.

SERVES 4

HAVE READY: food processor or liquidizer, electric or hand egg-whisk, ramekin or bowl.

4oz/100g slice from a round of
  goat's cheese
2 spring onions, finely sliced
freshly ground black pepper

1 tsp lemon juice
6oz/175g Quark
1 free-range egg-white

Place the ingredients (except the egg-white) in a food processor or
liquidizer and blend to a purée.
Whisk the egg-white until firm and stiff and fold into the mousse.
Place in a ramekin or bowl and serve.
If possible, chill before serving.

WHOLEMEAL WAFFLES

MAKES 4 WAFFLES

HAVE READY: sieve, electric or hand egg-whisk, saucepan (or
microwave dish) to melt margarine in, waffle-maker, fork.

4oz/100g wholemeal flour
1 tsp baking powder
2 free-range eggs, separated

¼pt/150ml skimmed milk
2oz/50g soft vegetable margarine,
  melted

Sift the flour with the baking powder into a mixing bowl.
Lightly beat the egg yolks with the milk.
Make a well in the centre of the flour and gradually add the egg and
milk, drawing the flour in from the sides of the well until you have a
smooth batter.
Fold in the melted margarine.
Whisk the egg-whites until firm and stiff.
Fold into the batter, using a metal tablespoon.
Heat the waffle-maker according to the manufacturer's instructions.
Place two tablespoonfuls of mixture in the base, close the lid and
cook for two minutes until golden brown.
Repeat until all the mixture is used up.
Serve hot, topped with a choice of cottage cheese and fruit, stewed
fruit, yoghurt, honey and lemon juice, carob or hazelnut spreads.

CHEESE AND ONION PANCAKES

SERVES 2–3
(extras will freeze)

HAVE READY: mixing bowl, sieve, fork, measuring jug, grater, omelette, crêpe or frying or pan, palette knife or fish-slice.

1 quantity basic batter (p. 204)	freshly ground black pepper
1 medium potato	pinch dry mustard
1 large onion	vegetable oil for frying
2oz/50g mature cheese, grated	

Make the batter in the usual way (p. 204).

Grate into it the scrubbed and peeled potato, onion and cheese.

Season to taste.

Heat the oil in the pan and when hot, but not smoking, add two tablespoonfuls of the batter.

Cook for 1½–2 minutes on one side, then flip over and cook the other side.

Repeat until all the mixture is used up.

Serve hot.

Note

Use as little oil as possible for frying. An oil-well which squeezes the brush to drain off oil helps cut down.

SPICED CASHEW SUPPER

This is a recipe based on Indian spiced vegetables but made with tofu instead of paneer – Indian curd cheese. (Paneer is also high in protein and low in fat but it takes a long time to make.)

SERVES 2

HAVE READY: garlic press, frying pan, fish-slice, or spatula.

1 tsp cumin seeds	½ tsp poppy seeds
1 tsp fennel seeds	4oz/100g green beans, sliced
4oz/100g roasted cashew pieces	¼pt/150ml natural yoghurt
1 tbsp vegetable oil	skimmed milk to moisten, if
1 aubergine, cubed	necessary
1 clove garlic, crushed	

Heat the frying pan until hot and toss in the cumin and fennel seeds and toast for a minute or two until they give off a delicious aroma, but are not burnt. Remove and toast the cashews. Remove these.

Cool the pan a little, then add the oil and the cubed aubergine and fry with the garlic and poppy seeds for ten minutes, stirring frequently.

Add the sliced beans, yoghurt and cashew pieces and cook over a low heat for fifteen minutes. If the mixture becomes too dry add a little skimmed milk.

BROCCOLI GRATIN

Cauliflower cheese is in danger of losing out to this new version which appears as a recipe meal in some frozen-food ranges but can be made very quickly at home. (Substitute cauliflower if you prefer the old favourite.)

SERVES 2

HAVE READY: two saucepans, wooden spoon, a measuring jug, grater, gratin dish.

4 large broccoli (or calabrese) spears
boiling water
1 tbsp wholemeal flour
1 tbsp vegetable oil

½pt/300ml skimmed milk
1 tsp meaux mustard
4oz/100g mature Cheddar cheese, grated
pinch paprika

Boil or steam the broccoli until just cooked but still retaining some bite (about five to seven minutes). Drain well.

Mix the flour and oil in a saucepan over a moderate heat to make a roux.

Gradually stir in the milk, cooking a little between additions.

Remove from the heat and stir in the mustard and all but a little cheese.

Place the broccoli in a gratin dish, cover with the sauce and top with the remaining cheese and paprika. Pass under a hot grill for a couple of minutes to melt and brown the cheese.

DOLMAS

MAKES ABOUT TEN PARCELS
(you will probably end up using a couple of leaves for
patching gaps or tears)

HAVE READY: large and small saucepan, frying pan, mixing
bowl, colander, dish with lid (if reheating).

10–12 large, green cabbage leaves
(Savoy)
4oz/100g bulgur/cracked wheat
1 onion
1 dsp vegetable oil

1 tsp each ground coriander, cumin
and garam masala
3oz/75g flaked almonds
1oz/25g currants

Wash the cabbage leaves well and blanch in boiling water for a
couple of minutes. Drain, then run under cold water to stop them
cooking.
Boil the bulgur for ten minutes in twice its volume of water which
should be absorbed during cooking. Drain if necessary.
Finely dice the onion and sauté in the oil and spices for five minutes.
Toast the almonds under a hot grill or in a hot pan, dry-heated.
Stir the bulgur, onion, nuts and currants together and place spoon-
fuls on the open leaves. Fold the leaves to make parcels enclosing the
filling.
Reheat, if required, in a pre-heated oven set to 350°F/180°C/Gas 4
(or microwave).

Note
Alternatively, vine leaves can be used (as they would in Greece or
Turkey), but the rather vinegary preserved ones available here are
not as tasty as fresh cabbage. You could also substitute pine kernels
for almonds, but the latter are slightly cheaper here. And for a change
use ½ tsp cinnamon instead of the Indian-style spices.

GARDEN-PEA OMELETTE

SERVES 2

HAVE READY: saucepan, fork or whisk, grater, omelette pan,
fish-slice or palette knife.

2oz/50g peas

3 free-range eggs

1oz/25g Gruyère cheese

freshly ground black pepper

corn (or soya) oil or unsalted butter

Boil the peas for five minutes or until cooked. Drain.

Lightly beat the eggs until frothy.

Heat the oil or butter in an omelette pan and pour in the egg mixture.

Carefully lift the edges as the omelette cooks and tip the pan to let liquid run beneath.

When almost set, add the peas and continue cooking.

Grate the cheese and sprinkle on top.

When set, either flash under a hot grill to melt the cheese or fold in half and serve.

PARSNIP CROQUETTES

MAKES 6 PATTIES

HAVE READY: a food processor or liquidizer, pastry board, frying pan.

1lb/450g parsnips

4oz/100g mature Cheddar, grated

freshly ground black pepper

1 tsp mustard powder

1 tbsp wholemeal flour (for board)

little vegetable oil

Peel and dice the parsnips. Boil until just cooked, but not too soft.

Place in a food processor or liquidizer with the cheese, pepper and mustard and blend to a purée.

When cool enough to handle, form into patty shapes on a lightly floured board.

Brush with vegetable oil and crisp each side quickly by popping into a heated, heavy-based frying pan.

Serve with peas and grilled tomatoes.

SALADS

SALAD PLATTER

SERVES 2

HAVE READY: saucepan (for the lentils), egg pan, screw-top jar, flat serving-platter.

4oz/100g brown/Puy lentils
2 hard-boiled free-range eggs
lots of crunchy lettuce (or endive)
2 carrots, grated
juice of half a lemon

2 tbsp olive oil
1 tbsp white wine vinegar
1 tsp meaux mustard
1 crushed clove garlic

Wash the lentils and boil in plenty of water for thirty minutes.
Bring the eggs to the boil and cook for seven to ten minutes.
Wash and shred the lettuce and place on the serving-platter.
Toss the grated carrots in the lemon juice.
Mix the remaining ingredients in a clean screw-top jar and shake vigorously to make the salad dressing.
Run the eggs under cold water and peel, then slice or quarter.
Drain the lentils, if necessary, and toss in the garlic dressing. Place on top of the lettuce and carrots. Garnish the edge of the platter with the eggs.

QUICK MUSHROOM SALAD

Also delicious as a toast-topper or pitta-bread filler with salad.

SERVES 2

HAVE READY: spatula, mixing bowl, serving bowl.

8oz/225g mushrooms
7oz/200g pot of hummus (or make your own p. 125)

juice of half a lemon
natural yoghurt, if liked

Slice the mushrooms into a mixing bowl.

Thin the hummus with the lemon juice and then toss the mushrooms in it.

If you like your salad a little 'wetter', you can add a tablespoon or two of natural yoghurt to the hummus mixture.

COLESLAW

SERVES 2
(with some left over for the lunchbox)

HAVE READY: food processor or grater, lemon squeezer, bowl to toss the salad in, serving bowl.

3oz/75g wedge white cabbage
2 carrots
2 sticks celery
1 small red apple
juice of half a lemon

½ green pepper
½ small onion (optional)
3 tbsp mayonnaise
freshly ground black pepper

Wash the cabbage and scrub the carrots. Pass through the fine-shredder on a food processor or grate by hand.

Slice the celery and dice the apple, tossing the apple in the lemon juice.

Dice the green pepper – and onion, if liked.

Mix all the ingredients together and blend in the remaining lemon juice, mayonnaise and pepper.

CHINESE CHEESE SALAD

HAVE READY: cheese plane, serving plate.

4oz/100g Edam (or Gouda) cheese
cos lettuce leaves
½ green pepper
1 kiwi fruit
1 tangerine or orange

4oz/100g green grapes, seedless if possible
1½ tbsp sunflower (or soya) oil
1 tbsp shoyu sauce
juice of an orange
freshly ground black pepper

Using a cheese plane, take slivers of cheese off a wedge of Edam (or Gouda) and roll them into little cones.

Shred the lettuce and slice the pepper and kiwi fruit.
Take segments from the tangerine (or orange) and halve and deseed the grapes.
Toss together the remaining ingredients to make a salad dressing.
Arrange the salad items on a serving plate and pour the dressing over them.

WINTER SALAD

This will make about 4–6 servings. It can be stored in the fridge and used as the basis of a meal, to accompany main dishes or put in the lunchbox.

HAVE READY: food processor or grater.

½ small white cabbage
2 carrots
1 eating apple
juice of half a lemon
2 sticks celery

1 onion
2oz/50g sultanas
2 heaped tbsp mayonnaise
freshly ground black pepper
3oz/75g chopped walnuts

Cut the cabbage into chunks and scrub or peel the carrots. Pass both through the grater on a food processor or grate by hand.
Core the apple, but do not peel. Finely dice and toss in the lemon juice.
Finely slice the celery and dice the onion.
Mix together all the ingredients.

Serve with a baked potato.

AVOCADO SALAD

SERVES 2
(as a light lunch)

HAVE READY: grapefruit knife, teaspoon, serving-dish.

1 large ripe avocado
juice of half a lemon
1 rose grapefruit

3.5oz/80g packet cashews (or 4oz/100g unsalted cashew pieces)

135

Peel the avocado. This is easily done by halving the fruit horizontally, then slipping the end of a teaspoon handle between fruit and skin – the skin should then peel off easily. Remove the stone by carefully impaling it on the knife point and then pulling out if it is a little bit reluctant to move. Slice the avocado into long strips and toss in the lemon juice.

Peel the grapefruit and remove the pith. (You can cut off the skin if you like but it is fiddly and takes a little while.) Using a serrated knife, cut out the segments and arrange these with the avocado slices.

Scatter the nuts over the mixture of grapefruit and avocado.

LAMB'S LETTUCE SALAD

This is quite easy to grow – even if you just have a window-box – and it's a lot cheaper than shop-bought, when available

SERVES 1–2

HAVE READY: salad shaker or colander, salad bowl, screwtop jar.

2 heads of lamb's lettuce	2 tbsp olive oil
1 small head of radicchio (or oak leaf lettuce)	¾ tbsp white wine vinegar
4oz/100g goat's cheese	freshly ground black pepper

Wash the lamb's lettuce and radicchio and dry well. Shred into a salad bowl. Crumble the goat's cheese over the top. Pour over a salad dressing, made by combining the remaining ingredients in a screwtop jar and shaking well.

ARTICHOKE SALAD

SERVES 2

HAVE READY: food flask or Thermos, two saucepans, egg-boiling pan, an egg-slicer, screw-top jar, serving-dish.

NIGHT BEFORE/MORNING: Soak the lentils in boiling water in a food flask or Thermos to reduce cooking time.

4oz/100g whole, green Continental
  lentils
1lb/450g new potatoes
2 free-range eggs
15oz/425g can artichoke hearts

2oz/50g stuffed green olives
2 tbsp olive oil
¾ tbsp wine vinegar
1 tsp meaux mustard
freshly ground black pepper

Boil the lentils in twice their volume of water for fifteen minutes.

Scrub the potatoes and boil for twelve to fifteen minutes until cooked but not mushy. Drain.

Boil the eggs for about seven minutes until hard-boiled. Drain, cool, shell and slice.

Drain the artichoke hearts – and the olives, if necessary.

Make the dressing by combining the remaining ingredients in a clean screw-top jar and shaking vigorously.

Toss the warm lentils in the dressing and pile in the centre of a serving-dish.

Arrange the potatoes, sliced eggs and artichoke hearts around the edge and scatter the olives on top.

CHICKPEA AND PASTA SALAD

SERVES 2

HAVE READY: egg-boiling pan, can-opener, saucepan, garlic press, screw-top jar, grater, serving-dish.

1 free-range egg
4oz/100g wholewheat pasta shapes
8oz/225g can chickpeas
1 onion
4 spring onions
1 clove garlic

2 tbsp olive oil
1 tbsp lemon juice
little lemon rind, grated
½ tsp ground cumin
fresh spinach leaves for serving
  (optional)

Boil the egg for about seven minutes until hard-boiled. Drain and cool, then shell and slice.

Boil the pasta in plenty of water, drain and then cool.

Drain the chickpeas.

Peel and slice the onion and dice the spring onions.

Crush the garlic and combine with the remaining ingredients in a clean screw-top jar and shake vigorously.

Toss all the salad ingredients together with the salad dressing.
Place on a bed of spinach leaves (if you like) on a serving-dish.

JAPANESE NOODLE SALAD

SERVES 2

HAVE READY: screw-top jar, saucepan, grater, colander.

1 packet Japanese Brown Rice
  Noodles*
3 small carrots
½ green pepper
2oz/50g mushrooms
¼ white radish or mooli

SHOYU SAUCE DRESSING
2 tbsp shoyu sauce
¾ tbsp brown rice vinegar
1 tbsp orange juice

Boil the noodles in plenty of water for four to five minutes (or as
instructed by manufacturer).
Drain and then chop into small pieces.
Grate half the carrots and cut the rest into julienne strips.
Slice the pepper and the mushrooms.
Grate the radish.
Toss all the ingredients together in the dressing, made in the screw-
top jar.

Serve at once while slightly warm.

Note
* Japanese noodles made from buckwheat and called ramen can also
be used. Sunwheel are the main importers in Britain and their
products are available in health-food shops.

CLASSIC THREE-BEAN SALAD

SERVES 2

HAVE READY: can-opener, two saucepans, screw-top jar,
colander, serving-dish.

4oz/100g red kidney beans, canned
4oz/100g white cannellini beans, canned
4oz/100g broad beans, frozen
3oz/75g wholemeal pasta shells, twists or rings

2 tbsp olive oil
¾ tbsp wine vinegar
1 tsp meaux mustard
freshly ground black pepper
1 tbsp freshly chopped parsley

Drain the kidney and cannellini beans.

Boil the broad beans for eight minutes (or according to the instructions on the pack).

Boil the pasta in plenty of water for about ten to twelve minutes (or according to instructions).

Drain the broad beans and pasta and mix them with the canned beans.

Make the dressing by combining the remaining ingredients (except the parsley) in a screw-top jar and shaking vigorously.

Toss the beans in the dressing, arrange on the serving-dish and garnish with parsley.

WARM POTATO SALAD

A salad to accompany other dishes.

HAVE READY: saucepan, colander, grater, serving-bowl.

1lb/450g small new potatoes
2 tbsp freshly chopped parsley

1 rounded tbsp mayonnaise
1oz/25g Gruyère cheese, grated

Scrub or scrape the potatoes and boil.

When just cooked, drain and place on one side.

Either use whole or cube and place in serving-bowl.

Toss in the rest of the ingredients. Serve warm.

CARROT AND NUT SALAD

SERVES 2

HAVE READY: grater, mixing bowl, screw-top jar.

6oz/175g carrots
3.5oz/80g packet Marks &
   Spencer's natural roasted
   unsalted peanuts

1 tbsp olive oil
⅓ tbsp white wine vinegar
freshly ground black pepper
½ tsp meaux mustard

Grate the carrots (or cut into julienne strips) and put in a mixing bowl with the nuts.

Place the rest of the ingredients in a clean, screw-top jar and shake vigorously.

Toss the carrots and nuts in the dressing.

WHITE BEAN SALAD

SERVES 1–2

HAVE READY: salad plate, egg-slicer, can-opener, serving-dish.

2 free-range eggs
½ crisp green lettuce
1 small onion
15oz/425g cannellini beans, canned

1 large beefsteak tomato, sliced
2oz/50g black olives
1 tbsp freshly chopped parsley

Boil the eggs for seven minutes until hard-boiled.

Drain and shell, when cool enough to handle.

Wash and shred the lettuce and dry well.

Place in the base of the serving-dish.

Peel and thinly slice the onion and layer on top of the lettuce.

Drain the beans and place them in a mound in the centre.

Slice the hard-boiled eggs and arrange, alternately with the slices of tomato, around the circumference.

Scatter the olives over the salad and top with the parsley.

GREEN BEAN SALAD

SERVES 2

HAVE READY: saucepan, screw-top jar, colander, serving-dish.

5oz/150g green beans
2oz/50g black olives (not pitted)
2oz/50g feta cheese, crumbled

VINAIGRETTE
2 tbsp olive oil

¾ tbsp wine vinegar
1 tsp méaux mustard
freshly ground black pepper

Wash the beans and top and tail them.
Blanch in boiling water for a couple of minutes, then run under cold water to stop them cooking.
Cut into smaller pieces – about three pieces from an average-size bean.
Place in a dish and toss in the vinaigrette (made in the screw-top jar).
Transfer to the serving-dish and sprinkle the olives and cheese over the top.

Serve with fresh, hot Granary rolls.

FETA SALAD

SERVES 2

HAVE READY: frying pan, absorbent kitchen paper, garlic press, serving-dish.

frisée or crisp lettuce leaves
bunch of watercress
cucumber

wholemeal croûtons
6oz/75g feta cheese, crumbled

Wash the lettuce and watercress and shake dry. Place in the base of the serving-dish.
Slice the cucumber and arrange on top of the lettuce.
Scatter over the top a generous portion of croûtons and the feta cheese.

CROÛTONS

With oil

To make these, cube some thick slices of wholemeal bread. Heat a couple of tablespoonfuls of olive oil in a frying pan with two cloves of crushed garlic and turn the cubes in the oil.

Drain on absorbent kitchen paper. Make the croûtons as crispy as you can without burning them.

Without oil

An alternative is to make croûtons without oil by heating a heavy-based frying pan and tossing the bread cubes in the pan so that they toast all over in a dry heat.

DRESSINGS

LOW-CALORIE MAYONNAISE

This is a pouring consistency. Reduce the amount of yoghurt to half for a thicker mayonnaise.

HAVE READY: mixing bowl, fork.

1 free-range egg yolk
1 tbsp olive oil
¼pt/150ml strained natural
  yoghurt

freshly ground black pepper
pinch mustard powder

Using a fork, lightly blend the egg yolk and oil into the yoghurt, then work in the seasoning.

VARIATIONS

Add the following for different flavoured mayonnaise:
- crushed garlic clove
- 1oz/25g mashed blue cheese
- freshly chopped herbs such as chives, parsley or dill
- juice of half a lemon

THOUSAND ISLAND DRESSING

1 tbsp sherry (or other dark)
   vinegar
1 tsp tomato purée
10–12 capers, finely chopped
2 tsp lemon juice

1 tbsp green pepper, very finely
   chopped
1 quantity basic low calorie
   mayonnaise

Make the mayonnaise on p. 142 and gently stir in all the ingredients.
Store in the fridge.

BLUE CHEESE DRESSING

2oz/50g Danish blue (or other soft
   blue cheese)

2 tsp lemon juice
1 quantity low calorie mayonnaise

Make the mayonnaise on p. 142 and carefully mash the cheese with
the lemon juice, then pour the mayonnaise on to it, stirring to blend
as you do so.

Note
If you prefer a ready-made mayonnaise, see p. 74.

MICROWAVE MIRACLES

Although there are many delicious vegetarian ready-meals to be bought (see pp. 75–6) the microwave also offers a good opportunity to speed up your general cooking in the kitchen. In this way, the microwave can mean that where previously you might not have felt like cooking, or thought that you did not have time to prepare something, now you do! Using the microwave as another cooker, instead of just a reheating appliance, you can make quick evening meals or lunches that previously would have taken you far longer to put together.

ONION SOUP

SERVES 2

HAVE READY: microwave oven-proof dish, grater, grill (optional), soup bowls or a serving-dish.

2 large onions	freshly ground black pepper
1oz/25g unsalted butter	4 rounds toasted French stick
1pt/600ml vegetable stock	2oz/50g Gruyère cheese, grated
1 tbsp brown sauce	

Finely slice the onions and place in a microwave oven-proof dish with the butter.

Cover and cook on HIGH for five minutes until the onions are very soft.

Add the stock and sauce, season with pepper and return to the oven on HIGH for a further eight minutes.

Pour into soup bowls or serving dish and top with the toast, sprinkled with grated cheese.

Return to the oven to melt the cheese for one minute on HIGH.

Note
Alternatively you can toast the bread and melt the cheese on it under

the grill, then place it French-style in the bottom of the soup bowls or serving-dish and pour the hot soup over it.

CORN AND CARROT CHOWDER

SERVES 2

HAVE READY: greaseproof paper, liquidizer or food processor, microwave oven-proof dish with lid, microwave oven-proof measuring jug.

2 corn on the cob	Tabasco
2 carrots	1 tbsp vegetable oil
½ red pepper	1 tbsp wholemeal flour
sea salt	½pt/300ml skimmed milk
freshly ground black pepper	

Wrap the corn in greaseproof paper and cook on HIGH for six minutes. Remove from the oven and scrape off the kernels.

Slice the carrots and pepper and cook in a dish with two tablespoonfuls of cold water, covered, on HIGH for eight minutes, stirring once.

Place the carrots, pepper, cooking water and seasoning in a liquidizer or food processor.

Place the oil and flour in an oven-proof jug and cook on MEDIUM for thirty seconds. Remove, stir and repeat.

Stir in the milk and cook for thirty-second periods, stirring in-between until thickened and cooked.

Add to the liquidizer and blend.

Return the liquid to the jug in two batches, stir in the sweetcorn kernels and reheat on HIGH for one minute.

NUTTY STUFFED PEPPERS

SERVES 1

HAVE READY: microwave oven-proof dish with lid.

1 green (or red) pepper	8 tbsp water
1 small onion	2 tbsp cracked wheat
1 stalk celery	1 tbsp freshly chopped parsley
1 tbsp mixed nuts	freshly ground black pepper
¼ stock cube	

Halve and deseed the pepper.
Finely dice the onion and celery and chop the nuts. Mix together in a
dish with a lid, with the stock cube, water and cracked wheat.
Cover and cook on HIGH for four minutes.
Remove from the oven and stir in the parsley and season. Fill the
pepper halves and return to the oven in the covered dish.
Cook on HIGH for three to four minutes.

BUTTERBEANS AU VIN

SERVES 2

HAVE READY: microwave oven-proof casserole with lid,
measuring jug, corkscrew, can-opener, sieve.

1 carrot	½pt/300ml water
1 onion	2 leeks
4 black peppercorns	8oz/225g whole smallish
2 bay leaves	mushrooms
1 bouquet garni (or sachet or	14oz/400g can butterbeans
capsule)	2 tsp arrowroot (optional)
½pt/300ml white wine	

Dice the carrot and onion and place in the casserole with the
peppercorns, bay leaves and bouquet garni.
Pour on the wine and water and cover. Cook on HIGH for five
minutes. Allow to stand while preparing the vegetables.
Wash and slice the leeks diagonally about 1½in/4cm long.
Wipe the mushrooms.
Drain the butterbeans.
Strain the vegetable stock you have made and pour it on to the
vegetables and beans in the casserole.
Add the second bay leaf, cover and cook on HIGH for five minutes.
Stir and cook for another two or three minutes.
If you like, you can thicken the sauce by stirring in the arrowroot
slaked in a tablespoonful of cold water. Return to the oven on
MEDIUM for a minute, stirring again after thirty seconds.

Note

Bouquet garni is made by placing a few parsley stalks, black pepper-corns, a sprig of thyme and a bay leaf in some muslin and tying with string.

CHO CHO PIE

Cho cho is a Caribbean vegetable that can be used in savoury and sweet dishes. It is slightly starchy and does not have a distinctive flavour. Use potato, if you prefer.

SERVES 2

HAVE READY: microwave oven-proof dish with lid and small pie dish, rolling pin, microwave oven-proof jug, fork.

NIGHT BEFORE/MORNING: Remove pastry from freezer.

8oz/225g packet wholemeal pastry
10oz/275g cho cho
1 small onion
4oz/100g mushrooms
1 stem broccoli
1 tbsp vegetable oil

1 tbsp wholemeal flour
⅓pt/200ml skimmed milk
1 tsp mustard
freshly ground black pepper
shake Worcestershire sauce

Roll out the pastry and line a small pie dish.
Then roll out the remainder and cut a lid.
Dice the cho cho and the onion and slice the mushrooms.
Break the broccoli into florets. Place the vegetables in a dish on HIGH and cook, covered, for five minutes.
Put the vegetables into the pie dish.
Make the sauce by cooking the oil and flour on MEDIUM for thirty seconds. Stir in the milk. Return for thirty-second periods on HIGH, stirring between, until thickened. Stir in the seasonings and pour over the vegetables.
Place the pie lid in position and return to the microwave on BAKE or MEDIUM for seven to ten minutes.
Glaze the top with skimmed milk and brown under the grill.

CRACKED WHEAT WITH SPINACH AND ALMONDS

SERVES 2–3

HAVE READY: microwave oven-proof dishes with lids, measuring jug.

4oz/100g cracked wheat/bulgur or pourgouri
½pt/300ml boiling water
8 oz/225g thawed frozen spinach (or 1lb/450g fresh, washed spinach)

2 tsp ground cumin
½ tsp ground cinnamon
1oz/25g currants
2oz/50g flaked almonds
juice of half a lemon

Place the cracked wheat in a dish with a lid and pour on the boiling water. Cover and cook on HIGH for 5½ minutes. Stir once during cooking.

Mix the remaining ingredients (except the lemon juice) and place in a dish with a lid. Cover and cook on HIGH for three minutes, stirring once.

Drain the cracked wheat, if necessary, and stir in the lemon juice. Top the spinach mixture with the wheat and return to the oven uncovered, to reheat for one minute on HIGH.

AUBERGINE HOTPOT

SERVES 2–3

HAVE READY: microwave oven-proof casserole with lid, can-opener, wooden spoon.

NIGHT BEFORE/MORNING: boil four potatoes and let them cool.

1 aubergine
1 leek
1 onion
1 tbsp vegetable oil
14oz/400g can brown beans

14oz/400g can tomatoes
sea salt
freshly ground black pepper
4 cold, cooked potatoes

Place the aubergine in the microwave oven on HIGH for five minutes.

148

Remove and when cool enough to handle, cut into slices or large chunks.

Meanwhile slice the leek, dice the onion, and place in a dish with a lid and cook on HIGH, covered, for five minutes.

Add the drained brown beans and stir well.

Add the tomatoes and the diced aubergine. Season and return to the microwave, uncovered, for five minutes on HIGH. Slice the potatoes and remove the dish from the microwave. Arrange the slices on top – hotpot fashion – and then return to the microwave oven on HIGH for four minutes to completely heat through.

MUSHROOM AND SPINACH LASAGNE

SERVES 2–3

HAVE READY: basin, microwave oven-proof measuring jug and dish with lid, lasagne serving- and cooking-dish.

1 tbsp vegetable oil
1 tbsp wholemeal flour
½pt/300ml skimmed milk
4oz/100g mushrooms, sliced
pinch paprika
4oz/100g frozen spinach (or 8 oz/225g washed fresh spinach)

2oz/50g Gruyère cheese, grated
1 small leek, diced
6 sheets oven-ready Record Fasta Pasta Lasagne
½oz/12g Gruyère, grated, for topping (optional)

Place the oil and flour in the jug. Stir and heat on MEDIUM for thirty seconds. Remove and stir, then repeat.

Stir in the milk and return to the oven for thirty-second periods, stirring in between each, until the sauce thickens.

Remove and stir in the mushrooms and paprika.

Thaw the frozen spinach in a dish with a lid on HIGH for four minutes, stirring and breaking up, if necessary. Or chop fresh spinach into a dish with a lid. Add the grated cheese and the finely diced leek and cook on HIGH for one minute.

Now assemble the lasagne by placing half the spinach in the base of a dish and cover with two sheets of lasagne. Top this with half the mushroom mixture and repeat, ending with the mushroom mixture. On top you can add a further ½oz/12g of grated Gruyère, if liked. Cook on HIGH for five to seven minutes.

STUFFED MUSHROOMS

SERVES 2

HAVE READY: microwave oven-proof flat dish and casserole with lid.

6 large flat mushrooms
2oz/50g mushrooms
2 sticks celery
1 small onion
1 tbsp vegetable oil

6oz/175g cottage (or other low-fat, soft white) cheese
1 free-range egg
freshly ground black pepper
pinch paprika or cayenne pepper

Place the large mushrooms in a flat dish that will fit into the microwave oven.

Chop the other mushrooms, celery and onion and place in a dish with a lid and cook on HIGH for three minutes.

Beat together the cheese, egg and seasoning and mix with the vegetables. Pile on top of the flat mushrooms.

Cook on HIGH for four minutes.

AUBERGINE 'MOUSSAKA'

HAVE READY: can-opener, two microwave oven-proof dishes with lids, grater.

1 large aubergine
2 cloves garlic
1 large onion
14oz/400g can tomatoes
2 tsp freshly chopped oregano (or 1 tsp dried)

freshly ground black pepper
2 free-range eggs
¼pt/150ml thick natural yoghurt
2oz/50g Gruyère cheese, grated

Slice the aubergine and place in a large dish with a lid and cook on HIGH for two minutes. Remove. Dice the garlic and onion and chop the tomatoes.

Place these, with the tomato juice, in a dish and cook on HIGH for five minutes, stirring once or twice.

Sprinkle the oregano and pepper over the aubergine slices.

Place the tomato mixture on top.

Beat together the eggs, yoghurt and cheese and pour over the vegetables.

Bake on MEDIUM for five minutes.

Remove and place under the grill for two minutes to brown the top.

CHESTNUT ROAST

SERVES 2

HAVE READY: can-opener, food processor or liquidizer or hand-grater, nutmeg grater, mixing bowl, microwave oven-proof terrine or baking dish.

NIGHT BEFORE: this dish is good served cold either with Winter Salad (p. 135) or Coleslaw (p. 134), so you could make it the night before.

8oz/225g canned chestnuts (whole or puréed)
1 large onion
2 thick slices wholemeal bread
2oz/50g ground almonds
1 tbsp freshly chopped parsley
1 free-range egg to bind
freshly ground black pepper
grating of nutmeg

If the chestnuts are whole, place them in a food processor or liquidizer and blend to a purée, or roughly chop them by hand.

Peel the onion and grate in the food processor (or by hand).

Crumb the bread in the food processor (or by hand).

Mix together all the ingredients and place in a glass or ceramic terrine or other deep dish from which you can cut slices of the loaf when cooked.

Place in the oven on HIGH for fifteen minutes.

Serve either with a salad or green vegetable such as sprouts or cabbage.

Note

If you are going to cook this in a conventional oven set the oven to 375°F/190°C/Gas 5. It will take about thirty-five minutes.

PUMPKIN CURRY

SERVES 2

HAVE READY: microwave oven-proof dish with lid, frying pan, spoon or fish-slice, can-opener.

8oz/225g pumpkin
2 green chillies
1 clove garlic, crushed
1 onion, diced
1 tsp each ground cumin and
  coriander

1 tbsp oil
7oz/200g can tomatoes
½pt/300ml vegetable stock
14oz/400g can white beans
1 tbsp freshly chopped coriander
  leaves

Put some brown rice on to cook before you start making the curry. Allow about 2oz/50g dry weight per person.

Peel and cube the pumpkin. Place in a dish with a lid and cook on HIGH for five minutes. Dice the chillies, garlic and onion and place in a frying pan with the spices and oil and cook, stirring well for five minutes.

Add the onion and spice mixture to the pumpkin, together with the tomatoes and stock and cook, uncovered, on HIGH for a further five minutes. Drain the can of beans and add half its contents to the pumpkin curry, reserving the remainder for another use. Return to the oven on HIGH for another five minutes. Stir in the coriander leaves, leaving a few for garnishing the dish.

Serve with plain boiled brown rice or, if you do not have time to wait for rice to cook, serve with wholemeal or Indian breads.

PIZZA SCONE

SERVES 2

HAVE READY: sieve, mixing bowl, grater, measuring jug, cheese plane, microwave oven-proof dish with lid, pizza dish or baking parchment.

8oz/225g wholemeal flour
1 tsp baking powder

2oz/50g soft vegetable margarine
1 tbsp grated Parmesan cheese

¼pt/150ml skimmed milk

TOPPING
1 red pepper, sliced

2 courgettes
1 onion, diced
3 tomatoes
4oz/100g Mozarella cheese

Sift the flour and baking powder into a mixing bowl and rub in the margarine.

Stir in the cheese and the milk to make a soft dough. Shape it into a round and place on baking parchment or a ceramic pizza dish, making an indentation in the centre to accommodate the filling. To make this, slice the pepper and courgettes, dice the onion and chop the tomatoes.

Place the vegetables in a dish with a lid and cook on HIGH for five minutes, stirring twice.

Spread the mixture over the top of the scone and then cut thin slices of cheese with a cheese plane to put on top of the filling.

Place in the oven on MEDIUM or BAKE and cook for fifteen minutes.

STUFFED COURGETTES

SERVES 2

HAVE READY: food processor or liquidizer, grater, microwave oven-proof dish with lid.

4 good-sized courgettes
1 onion
1 clove garlic
2 tomatoes
2oz/50g mixed chopped nuts

1oz/25g wholemeal breadcrumbs
freshly ground black pepper
1 dsp freshly chopped parsley
2oz/50g cheese, grated

Halve the courgettes lengthwise and scoop out the flesh.

Place the flesh in a food processor or liquidizer with the roughly chopped onion, garlic and tomatoes and blend.

Stir in the nuts and breadcrumbs.

Stuff the courgette halves with the mixture.

Place them in a dish with a lid and sprinkle over the pepper, parsley and cheese and cook on HIGH for seven minutes.

Remove and place under a hot grill for two or three minutes.

FENNEL CASSEROLE

SERVES 2

HAVE READY: microwave oven-proof dish with lid, jug and serving-dish, garlic press, grater, measuring jug, wooden spoon, serving-dish.

2 large bulbs of fennel
1 onion
2 cloves garlic
4 ripe tomatoes
freshly ground black pepper
1 tbsp wholemeal flour

1 tbsp vegetable oil
¼pt/150ml skimmed milk
1½oz/40g mature Cheddar-style cheese
½ tsp dried dill

Scrub the fennel and cut each bulb lengthways into three or four slices. Place in a dish with a lid and add four tablespoons of water. Cook on HIGH for five minutes. Drain, reserving the fennel liquid. Dice the onion, crush the garlic, chop the tomatoes, sprinkle with pepper and cook on HIGH for five minutes, stirring once. Place the flour and oil in a jug and cook on MEDIUM for thirty seconds. Stir and repeat. Remove and stir in the milk and fennel liquid. Then return to the oven for periods of thirty seconds on HIGH, stirring between until the sauce is thick. Then remove and stir in the cheese. Place the fennel in the base of a microwave oven-proof serving-dish, top with the tomato mixture. Sprinkle over the dill and top with the sauce. Return to the oven on HIGH for five minutes.
Flash under a hot grill to brown, if liked.

PARSNIP AND TOMATO BAKE

SERVES 2

HAVE READY: peeler, microwave oven-proof dish with lid, grater.

1lb/450g parsnips
10oz/275g tomatoes
3oz/75g mature Cheddar-style cheese

½oz/12g freshly chopped parsley
1½oz/40g fresh wholemeal breadcrumbs
freshly ground black pepper

Peel and slice the parsnips and layer in a dish.

Pour over four tablespoonfuls of water and cook, covered, on HIGH for eight minutes, turning once to ensure even cooking.

Slice the tomatoes.

Grate the cheese and mix with the parsley and breadcrumbs.

Remove the parsnips from the oven and layer the dish with half the parsnips, topped by half the tomatoes and then half the cheese.

Repeat, reserving a little cheese for topping.

Return to the oven, covered, on HIGH for five minutes, then stand for three minutes.

Transfer to beneath the grill with the reserved cheese sprinkled on top and brown.

GOULASH WITH NOODLES

SERVES 4

HAVE READY: microwave oven-proof casserole with lid, garlic press, teaspoon, wooden spoon, measuring jug.

1 onion, diced
1 clove garlic, crushed
2 courgettes, sliced
1 tsp caraway seeds
1 tsp dried marjoram
1 tsp paprika
2 carrots, in julienne strips
3 ripe tomatoes, chopped

8oz/225g white cabbage, shredded
1pt/600ml vegetable stock
2 tsp arrowroot
1 tsp tomato purée
4oz/100g strained Greek yoghurt
paprika for garnish
6oz/175g fettucine *verde* (or tagliatelle)

Place the onion, garlic and courgettes in a large microwave casserole with a lid.

Add the spices and herbs and cook, covered, for five minutes, stirring once.

Meanwhile blanch the carrots and cabbage in a little boiling water and drain, reserving the liquid which can then be made up to the pint of vegetable stock.

Add the cabbage and carrots to the other vegetables with the stock and return to the microwave on HIGH for fifteen minutes.

Slake the arrowroot in a little water and stir in the tomato purée.

Remove the dish from the oven and add a little of the hot liquid to the arrowroot, then return to the dish and stir.

Return to the microwave on HIGH for thirty-second periods, stirring between, until thickened. Remove and just before serving stir in the yoghurt, leaving visible swirls over which you can sprinkle a pinch of paprika.

Serve with the noodles.

Note

Boil the pasta in twice its volume of water either on the hob while the goulash is cooking or leave the goulash to stand, covered, and cook the pasta on HIGH for about twelve minutes or four if it's fresh pasta.

BEAN POTS

SERVES 2

HAVE READY: microwave oven-proof dish with lid, can-opener, potato masher, grater, a measuring jug, two ramekins.

2 large potatoes
2–3 tbsp skimmed milk
2oz/50g mature cheddar-style cheese, grated

14oz/400g can baked beans (or Batchelor's Bean Cuisine or Whole Earth Campfire Beans)
2 tomatoes

Scrub or peel the potatoes and chop roughly.

Place in a microwave dish with a lid and cover.

Cook on HIGH for ten–twelve minutes, or until soft. Drain. Mash the potatoes with the milk and stir in the grated cheese.

Place the beans in two ramekins and top each with a sliced tomato.

Place the mashed potato on top and return to the oven on HIGH for two to three minutes.

Flash under a hot grill to brown, if liked.

PAK CHOI WITH ALMONDS

SERVES 2

HAVE READY: microwave oven-proof casserole with lid, measuring jug, tablespoon, teaspoon, colander, can-opener, grill or hot pan to toast the almonds.

4–6 pak choi (or Chinese leaves)
6 spring onions, sliced
4oz/100g mushrooms, sliced
2 carrots, in julienne strips
½ green pepper, thinly sliced
5–7oz/150–200g can bamboo
   shoots
4oz/100g beansprouts
3oz/75g flaked almonds, toasted

SAUCE
4 tbsp water
2 tsp arrowroot
4 tbsp shoyu sauce
1 tbsp tomato ketchup
1 tbsp sherry

Cut the leaves across into strips and prepare the rest of the vegetables.

Place them all, except the beansprouts, in a large microwave oven-proof casserole with a lid and cook on HIGH for five minutes, stirring once to ensure even cooking. Make the sauce by gradually stirring the water into the arrowroot, then adding the rest of the liquids.

Add the sauce and the beansprouts and cook for a further four minutes, stirring once, and serve with the almonds sprinkled over the top of the vegetables.

GREEN BEANS AND CASHEWS

SERVES 1

HAVE READY: microwave oven-proof dish with lid, clean screw-top jar

8oz/225g green (or French) beans
6 tbsp water
2oz/50g cashew nut pieces

1 tbsp olive oil
2 tsp wine vinegar
freshly ground black pepper

Top and tail the beans and place in a dish with a lid, together with the water. Cover and cook on HIGH for six to eight minutes or until the beans are cooked but still slightly firm. Remove and drain, if necessary.

Lightly toast the nuts in a grill pan and then toss over the beans.

Mix together the oil, wine vinegar and pepper in a jar and pour over the beans and cashews. Serve warm.

QUICK RATATOUILLE

SERVES 2

HAVE READY: microwave oven-proof dish with lid.

4 ripe tomatoes	2 courgettes
1 onion	1 tbsp mixed fresh herbs (or 1 tsp
½ green pepper	dried)
½ red pepper	2 tbsp vinaigrette

Slice all the vegetables finely and place in a dish with a lid. Cover and cook on HIGH for eight minutes, stirring twice during the cooking. Remove from the heat and stir in the vinaigrette.

Serve with some Parmesan cheese to sprinkle over and wholemeal rolls.

POTATO SKINS WITH MUSHROOM FILLING

SERVES 2

Crispy potato skins are served as a snack or starter in many American restaurants, but they seem to be rather an over-priced (and over-rated) item. However, made at home, with a creamy mushroom filling, they're a different matter . . . This recipe uses a combination of microwave and standard oven (or grill).

HAVE READY: microwave oven-proof dish, liquidizer or food processor, potato masher.

2 × 8oz/225g baking potatoes	freshly grated nutmeg
8oz/225g mushrooms	4 tbsp skimmed milk
1oz/25g unsalted butter	freshly chopped parsley
pinch paprika	

Set the oven to 400°F/200°C/Gas 6 or heat the grill.

Scrub the potatoes, pierce the skins and cook on HIGH in the microwave oven for about twelve minutes.
Remove and allow to cool a little.

Chop the mushrooms and place in a dish with the butter. Cover and cook on HIGH for two minutes.

Transfer to a liquidizer or food processor and add the paprika and nutmeg.

Halve the potatoes and scoop out the flesh.

Place the potato shells in the standard oven or under the grill to crisp for ten to fifteen minutes.

Transfer half the potato flesh to the mushroom mixture and blend to a purée.

Mash the remaining potato with the milk to a creamy consistency.

Line the skins with a layer of plain mashed potato and fill the centre with the mushroom mixture.

Garnish with chopped parsley.

CABBAGE AND LEEK PARCELS

SERVES 2
(makes 4 parcels)

HAVE READY: microwave oven-proof dish with lid (or saucepan), measuring jug, grater, pastry brush, baking sheet.

NIGHT BEFORE/MORNING: defrost the sheets of filo pastry.

8oz/225g green cabbage (Savoy)	½ tbsp skimmed milk
1 large leek (about	1 tsp dried dill
8–9oz/225–250g)	little vegetable oil
freshly grated nutmeg	6 sheets filo pastry
½ tbsp wholemeal flour	oil, milk or egg to glaze

Set the oven to 350°F/180°C/Gas 4.

Shred the cabbage and cut the leek into small strips. Season with nutmeg.

Place in a dish with lid and cook on HIGH for eight minutes, stirring from time to time to ensure even cooking. (Alternatively blanch in saucepan on the hob for five minutes.)

Place the flour and milk in a jug and cook on MEDIUM for thirty seconds. Remove, stir and repeat. (Alternatively make a roux in the saucepan.)

Remove and stir in the milk. Return and cook for thirty-second periods on HIGH, stirring between until thickened.

Add the dill, then stir the cabbage mixture into the sauce.

Place three layered sheets of filo pastry on a floured, flat surface and cut in half. Place a quarter of the cabbage mixture on each half and lightly oil the edges of the pastry. Bring the edges up into a twist at the top to seal, folding them like sheets of paper. Repeat with the remaining three sheets of filo.

Place on a baking tray and lightly oil (or glaze with milk or egg-wash) and then bake for fifteen minutes until golden brown. Serve hot.

SPINACH PANCAKES

This is an old favourite and a very handy dish for a light meal and for freezing.

SERVES 4

HAVE READY: Items for making pancakes, if starting from scratch (p. 204), microwave oven-proof dish with lid and a gratin, saucepan, food-processor or liquidizer, wooden spoon, grater.

NIGHT BEFORE/MORNING: Make or defrost about eight pancakes.

1 quantity of wholemeal pancakes	1 tbsp vegetable oil
1lb/450g fresh spinach (or 8oz/225g frozen spinach, thawed)	¼ pt/150ml skimmed milk
	freshly grated nutmeg
	freshly ground black pepper
1 tbsp wholemeal flour	2oz/50g Gruyère cheese

Set the oven to 350°F/180°C/Gas 4, if you are going to heat the pancakes in a conventional oven.

Make, or defrost and warm, the pancakes.

Wash the fresh spinach and cook in a covered dish in the microwave on HIGH for two minutes (or cook fresh spinach in a saucepan, without additional water, turning frequently). Chop the spinach in the food processor or liquidizer or by hand.

Make a roux in the microwave by combining the flour and oil in a jug and cooking on MEDIUM for thirty seconds. Stir and repeat. Stir in the milk, then return for thirty-second periods on HIGH, stirring in between, until the sauce is thickened. (Or stir together the flour and oil in the saucepan over a moderate heat to make a roux. Gradually add the milk to make a thick sauce.)

Stir the spinach into the sauce and season with nutmeg and pepper. Combine the cheese with the sauce.

Fill the pancakes with the spinach and cheese filling, roll up and reheat in the microwave (or sprinkle the cheese *over* the pancakes and place under a hot grill in a gratin dish until the cheese has melted).

VEGETARIAN LUNCHBOXES

I love thick wholemeal sandwiches in my lunchbox, but not everyone does and there are times when you run out of fillings and ideas for them. The following suggestions are designed to give you other ideas for packing your lunchbox.

There is no doubt that sandwiches are cheaper, so if you're on a tight budget you could use one of these 'alternatives' as a treat each week. Or if you are really into exotic non-sandwich lunchboxes, start at the beginning here and work straight through . . .

A SALAD A DAY . . .

Pack up a salad from the selection on pp. 133–41. Accompany it with any of the following: pitta bread, wholemeal bread(s) and rolls, crackers and crispbread.

GO FRENCH WITH *PAN BAGNA*

Buy a French stick and cut it into quarters for the family or friends to make a *Pan Bagna* which you can fill with: shredded lettuce, onion rings, sliced tomatoes, sliced red pepper, black olives and hard-boiled egg. Spread the bread with a little olive oil (instead of butter or margarine) *or* take some dressing in a little jar (the hotel breakfast-preserve jars are handy for lunchboxes) and pour over just before eating.

JUST A SNACK

Get yourself a Vessen snack-pack from the health-food shop or delicatessen (even supermarkets have them). It's a pack of oatmeal biscuits with individual tubs of vegetable pâté and three varieties to choose from. Pack in some fresh fruit and you're away . . .

CRANKS' BAP

If you're not lucky enough to work near a branch of this vegetarian restaurant and takeaway chain then you will have to defrost a homemade Cheese Bap (p. 211). Fill it with either grated carrot or mustard and cress for a taste of the real thing.

SAMPLE A SAMOSA

If you usually run to the deli to get a samosa for lunch (and sometimes get the meat ones mistakenly), then there will be no confusion with the Vegetable Samosa in 'Cooking Ahead' p. 200. Take a napkin with you, but you will find these samosas are nowhere near as oily as the bought versions. Follow up with a cooling yoghurt – a no-additives real fruit one or perhaps natural yoghurt with a piece of fresh fruit.

THE LATE, LATE BREAKFAST LUNCH

You don't have to eat muesli only for breakfast. It is designed to eat at any time of the day. So, pick up a snack-pot of muesli or take your own – with a separate bottle of milk or put the muesli in a container with a good seal and let it soak all morning in skimmed milk, water, or fruit juice and water. Chop up some fresh fruit such as a banana, apple or peach and stir in just before you eat.

MEXICAN MOMENT

If you are tempted to rush to the pub for a bag of crisps and a pint, then the next best thing is a bag of tortilla chips, which you can dip into a pot of hummus bought in your lunch-hour or homemade (p. 125). Or you might have some leftover Brown Bean Pâté or Aubergine Pâté (pp. 126, 186). It's a rather salty lunch, so take some juice and lots of fresh fruit or yoghurt for pud. If you want an alcohol-free beer, Clausthaler is the *only* acceptable one, I think.

CRUDITÉS

If you don't fancy the idea a salad or don't have time to make one the morning, you can always pop a few raw vegetables in a lunchbox and take a knife/peeler to work (or keep one in your desk) to make some crudités at lunchtime. Eat with pâtés (see last entry) or pop to the shops for a tub of hummus or tzatziki (yoghurt, cucumber and herbs).

NOT QUITE CORNISH

This isn't an invitation to a double cream tea but a suggestion that a Vegetable Pastie (p. 199) could make a good lunchbox filler. It's quite filling, so you will probably only need some fruit afterwards.

SWEET OR SAVOURY SCONES

Either of these is good for the lunchbox. Cheese ones (p. 207) make a good main meal in the lunchbox with some tomatoes or other raw vegetables and sultana ones (p. 206) are better than a sticky bun if, like Winnie-the-Pooh, you can't do without 'a little something' at elevenses.

FLANS

You can buy a slice of flan or make your own. Choose flans with lower-fat fillings: if you are making one then choose a lower-fat cheese (or use a little strongly flavoured cheese) and use natural yoghurt instead of cream. Fill the flan with vegetables like leeks, courgettes, tomatoes, onions and mushrooms or even add cold, cooked beans and lentils to the fillings to bulk out with fibre and nutrients rather than with fat. Take some raw vegetables or some fruit with the flan.

RICE IS NICE

If you have cold leftover rice from the night before, you can stir in some Bombay Mix to make a spicy rice salad or some chopped fresh veg of your choice, cold beans or other pulses. Add a little French dressing and remember to pack a fork.

AVOCADO

Take a half or whole avocado, a wedge of lemon, some slices of bread (or a small pot of cottage cheese), and you have an ideal lunch.

VEGGIE SCOTCH EGG

This is a substantial lunch. You may be able to buy a scotch egg at your local health-food shop or you can make your own (p. 106). Again, tomatoes and other raw vegetables make a good accompaniment. You could even take some veggie ketchup in a small bottle.

Nut rissoles (p. 98), and burgers or patties (pp. 109, 124) are good alternatives to scotch eggs. They are tasty cold and make good solo or salad meals.

SIMON'S SPECIAL

I once worked with a chap called Simon who went through a phase of eating virtually nothing but bananas for lunch. When he wasn't eating these, he had a litre pot of natural yoghurt into which he stirred something crunchy like Jordans Original granola cereal . . . Add a few slices of banana to make this even better.

CONTINENTAL LENTILS

If you have tolerant working colleagues they will not mind the pungent aroma of cold continental lentils with garlic. The whole green lentils are cooked until just soft and while still warm are tossed in vinaigrette to which two or three crushed garlic cloves have been added. Eat with toast or, for a packed lunch, any kind of wholemeal or other grain bread.

CUP OF SOUP

Not the instant, just-add-boiling-water type but a Thermos of homemade soup. Choose from any of the varieties on pp. 175–9. You can defrost and heat the soup in the morning in the microwave and pour it into the vacuum flask. Take a bread roll or some crispbread to crumble over the top. Don't forget a spoon if you don't like drinking soup.

BAKED BEAN HOT POT

This one takes a little, but not a lot of, preparation. Finely dice an onion and half an eating apple and heat them in the microwave for a

165

couple of minutes to soften. Heat a small can of baked beans and stir in the apple and onion, plus a handful of raisins, if liked, and pop in a food flask. You might also like a dash of Tabasco or vegetarian Worcestershire sauce.

LUNCHBOX TREATS

There are some alternatives to standard fatty and salty crisps available for the occasional lunchbox treat and these are on pp. 45–6. (As an on-the-spot reminder they are: low fat or salt crisps, wholewheat crisps, Wheat Eats and tortilla and corn chips.)

And from the 'Cooking Ahead' section (pp. 199–211) you could add one of the following: malt loaf, flapjack, rich fruit bread, banana bread, sultana scones or digestive biscuits.

EVERYDAY ITEMS

Each day you could include some of the following: fruit, raw vegetables, yoghurt, fruit juice or mineral water.

FASTA PASTA

The British, traditionally eating potatoes, tend to forget about pasta. Pasta is much quicker to cook than potatoes and is just as good for you as the basis of a high-fibre, low-fat diet. This section includes recipes for wholemeal and *verde* (green) pasta as a jumping-off point. Start experimenting for yourself with the different sauces and accompaniments. And don't forget you can also use pasta in place of potatoes to accompany main dishes.

You have probably heard of the term *al dente*. It means cooking pasta until it is soft but still offering some resistance or 'bite' when cooked. It's important not to overcook the pasta because it then goes soggy and isn't half as nice ... Wholemeal pasta cooks in about twelve minutes and you will need about 3oz/75g each for a main meal. Fresh pasta is more delicious and cooks quicker. It is sold in 9oz/250g packs. Follow the manufacturer's instructions and serve about 4oz/100g per person. You can freeze what you don't use or cook it all and have a pasta salad later in the week. Simply make the Quick Mushroom Salad (p. 133) and toss in the leftover pasta – chopped, if necessary.

PASTA 'N' PESTO

This pesto is made without basil leaves.

SERVES 2

HAVE READY: pestle and mortar, garlic press, large saucepan, colander.

1oz/25g pine kernels
2 cloves garlic, crushed
1–2oz/25–50g Parmesan cheese, grated
juice of a lemon

freshly ground black pepper
3fl oz/90ml olive oil
6–8oz/175–225g pasta of your choice

167

Crush the pine kernels with the pestle and mortar.

Crush the garlic in a garlic press and pound together with the pine kernels.

Stir in the cheese, lemon juice and seasoning.

Trickle in the oil to make a thick paste.

Boil the pasta (spaghetti, tagliatelle, shells, penne or any shape you like) until *al dente*. Drain.

Toss the pasta in the pesto.

SPAGHETTI ITALIANO!

SERVES 2

HAVE READY: large and medium-size saucepans, grater, colander.

6oz/175g wholemeal spaghetti
1 jar Whole Earth Italiano! sauce
1 tbsp basil or parsley, freshly chopped (optional)

2 carrots, grated (optional)
Parmesan cheese, served separately

Boil the spaghetti in a large saucepan in plenty of water for ten to twelve minutes if dried or for about four if fresh (or according to manufacturer's instructions).

Heat the Italiano! Sauce in the second saucepan.

Drain the pasta and either pour the sauce over individual servings on plates or toss the pasta in a serving bowl with the sauce.

Alternatively you can enhance the Italiano! sauce by stirring in the herbs and grated carrot. Do not cook for long to leave them crunchy. Serve with Parmesan.

TWO QUICK SPAGHETTIS FOR ONE

HAVE READY: large and medium-size saucepans, garlic press, colander.

1 onion, diced
2 cloves garlic
1 tbsp olive oil

freshly ground black pepper
freshly chopped parsley

Sauté the diced onion and crushed garlic in olive oil for about five minutes.
Toss the cooked and drained spaghetti in the mixture.
Sprinkle with black pepper and freshly chopped parsley.

HAVE READY: large and medium-size saucepans, garlic press, colander.

1oz/25g unsalted butter or olive oil
2 cloves garlic
2 tbsp Parmesan cheese, grated

Heat the butter or oil in a saucepan and add the crushed garlic. Sauté for about five minutes until softened.
Toss the cooked and drained spaghetti in the sauce and sprinkle with Parmesan cheese.

FOUR CHEESES FOR TWO

HAVE READY: large and medium-size saucepans, grater, cheese plane, colander.

1oz/25g Parmesan cheese   1oz/25g Emmental cheese
1oz/25g Gruyère cheese   1oz/25g Mozarella cheese

Grate the first three cheeses and toss the cooked and drained spaghetti in them.
Slice the Mozarella thinly, cut into strips and stir into the pasta.

AND ALSO

You can serve tagliatelle or tagliolini with the same sauces and dressings as spaghetti. Tagliolini (also called *paglia e fieno*) is a very fine pasta, thinner than spaghetti, available from Pasta Reale or from fresh pasta shops.

MUSHROOM AND PISTACHIO TAGLIATELLE

SERVES 2

HAVE READY: large and two medium-size saucepans, grater, colander.

4oz/100g button mushrooms
4 tbsp vegetable stock
1 tbsp wholemeal flour
1 tbsp vegetable oil
⅓pt/200ml skimmed milk
freshly ground black pepper

sea salt
2oz/50g pistachio nuts (shelled weight)
8oz/225g green tagliatelle
Parmesan cheese, offered separately

Place the mushrooms in a saucepan with the stock and cook slowly for five minutes.

In another saucepan mix the flour and oil to make a roux. Gradually stir in the milk, cooking between additions to make a smooth sauce. Season, then stir in the nuts and drained mushrooms.

Boil the fresh pasta in the large saucepan for three to four minutes (or about seven to eight if dried – or according to the manufacturers' instructions), so that it is ready when the sauce is cooked.

Drain the pasta and arrange on individual plates and pour over the sauce.

Serve with grated Parmesan.

FETA PASTA

SERVES 2

HAVE READY: large and medium-size saucepans, ramekin (or bowl) for the cheese, colander.

1 medium onion, diced
2 cloves garlic, crushed
½ red pepper, diced
½ green pepper, diced
1 tbsp olive oil
14oz/400g can peeled plum tomatoes
8oz/225g mushrooms, sliced

freshly ground black pepper
pinch dry basil (or ½ tbsp fresh, finely chopped)
5oz/150g fresh wholemeal tagliatelle
freshly chopped parsley
black olives for garnish
3oz/75g crumbly feta cheese

Place the onion, garlic and peppers in a saucepan with the oil and cook over a gentle heat, stirring from time to time, for five minutes.

Add the tomatoes and break them up with the back of a wooden spoon and continue cooking for five minutes.

Stir in the sliced mushrooms and seasoning and continue cooking for ten minutes.

Boil the pasta in plenty of water for twelve minutes (or as instructed on the pack).

Place the drained pasta on plates. Garnish the sauce with chopped parsley or toss in a few black olives.

Offer the sauce with feta cheese separately.

RED HOT PASTA

SERVES 2

HAVE READY: garlic press, large and medium-size saucepans, colander.

3 chillies
2 cloves garlic
1 tbsp vegetable oil
4 large ripe tomatoes

2oz/50g mushrooms, sliced
1 tbsp fresh parsley
4oz/100g wholemeal pasta spirals, shells or other shapes

Chop the chillies finely and crush the garlic.

Place in a pan with the oil and cook for five minutes to soften but not brown.

Add the tomatoes and break them up with the back of a wooden spoon as the mixture cooks.

Stir in the sliced mushrooms and cover.

Continue to cook for another ten minutes, stirring from time to time to prevent the sauce sticking to the pan or burning.

Stir in the parsley just before serving.

Toss the cooked and drained pasta in the sauce or, if you prefer, top the pasta with it.

TAGLIATELLE AND TOMATO SAUCE

SERVES 2

HAVE READY: garlic press, large and medium-size saucepans, liquidizer or food processor, colander.

3 cloves garlic
1 large onion
1 tbsp vegetable oil
14oz/400g can tomatoes
pinch dried basil and oregano

freshly ground pepper
5oz/150g fresh tagliatelle
1 tbsp fresh parsley, chopped
Parmesan cheese, served separately

Crush the garlic and finely chop the onion.

Place in a saucepan with the oil and cook with the lid on for about ten minutes until soft.

Add the tomatoes and break them up with the back of a wooden spoon.

Stir in the herbs (except parsley) and seasoning and cook for a further five minutes.

Liquidize and return to the pan to heat through.

Cook the pasta in plenty of boiling water for the time specified on the pack. Drain.

Stir the parsley into the sauce just before serving.

Serve with Parmesan, if liked.

CRUNCHY CANNELLONI

SERVES 2

HAVE READY: large saucepan, bowl, colander.

8 large cannelloni tubes
6oz/175g lebne (yoghurt cheese)
2in/5cm piece cucumber
½ green pepper

4 spring onions
2 tsp lemon juice
freshly ground black pepper

Boil the pasta tubes in plenty of water according to the manufacturer's instructions, then drain.

Place the lebne in a bowl.

Dice the cucumber and pepper and slice the spring onions.

Mix the vegetables and lebne with lemon juice and black pepper. Stuff the warm tubes. Serve at once.

Note

If you do not have cannelloni, or cannot get green pasta, then you can make your own by blanching sheets of lasagne and rolling them to make cannelloni.

PINE KERNEL PASTA

SERVES 2–3

HAVE READY: large and medium-size saucepans, colander.

6oz/175g fresh, washed spinach
2oz/50g Parmesan cheese
2oz/50g pine kernels

5oz/150g tagliolini
freshly ground black pepper

Shred the washed spinach into a saucepan and cook for three minutes with no added water. Add the Parmesan and pine kernels and continue cooking, covered, for five minutes. Boil the pasta for three minutes (or as instructed on the pack) and drain.
Toss the spinach sauce with the pasta and season with freshly ground black pepper.

TORTELLONI WITH TOMATO SAUCE

SERVES 2

HAVE READY: large and medium-size saucepans, grater, garlic press, can-opener, colander.

8oz/250g pack fresh tortelloni
  (with ricotta cheese and spinach
  filling)
2 shallots

1 clove garlic
½ tbsp olive oil
7oz/200g can tomatoes
Parmesan cheese, served separately

Boil the tortelloni in plenty of water for ten to twelve minutes (or as instructed on the pack). Finely dice the shallots, crush the garlic and sauté them in the oil for a couple of minutes to soften.

Add the tomatoes and break them up with the back of a wooden spoon. Continue cooking over a moderate heat for about ten minutes.

Drain the pasta and place in serving bowls. Spoon over the sauce and serve at once with Parmesan cheese, if liked.

AND ALSO

Tortelloni is also good just cooked and tossed in freshly grated Parmesan.

For another flavour, try adding finely chopped sage leaves, black pepper and Parmesan to your bowl of steaming hot tortelloni.

Soups

Soup is an extraordinarily useful food. It can make a quick meal for lunch or supper and the Japanese even eat miso soup for breakfast. While soup is very versatile, it is also something that people have strong likes and dislikes about. Personally, I do not like soup that is remotely oily or fatty and enjoy soups that are creamy and thick in texture. Others prefer light consommés or broth-style soups with the vegetables visible. In this case I would suggest that you don't liquidize the soup where I have suggested you do so. Similarly, some people may prefer their soup thinner, so increase the amount of vegetable stock or other liquid used according to taste.

The servings are based on soup as a complete meal, so if you are using the recipes as part of a larger meal you may find they serve more people than stated.

Note
There are also soup recipes in the microwave section.

Cucumber Boursin Soup

SERVES 2

HAVE READY: measuring jug, liquidizer or food processor, soup bowls.

1 cucumber
½ small Boursin (or low-fat herb cheese)
5oz/150g strained Greek yoghurt

½pt/300ml vegetable stock
freshly ground black pepper
fresh mint for garnish

Scrub the cucumber and chop roughly.
Place in a liquidizer or food processor with the rest of the ingredients and blend to a fine purée.
Pour into soup bowls and garnish with chopped mint or sprigs.

BROWN BEAN SOUP

SERVES 2

HAVE READY: food flask or Thermos, measuring jug, saucepan.

NIGHT BEFORE/MORNING: soak the beans in a food flask or Thermos of boiling water.

4oz/100g brown beans, soaked
1 leek
2 sticks celery
1 onion
1 tbsp olive oil

1 tbsp Worcestershire sauce
1 tbsp shoyu sauce
2 tbsp Kensington (or other brown sauce)
¾pt/450ml vegetable stock (or water)

Drain the soaked beans and boil for forty minutes in fresh water.
Slice the leek into strips, the celery into slices and dice the onion.
Place the vegetables in a saucepan with the oil and sweat, covered, for about ten minutes, stirring from time to time.
Add the sauces, the stock and the drained beans and simmer for a further twenty-five minutes.

WATERCRESS SOUP

SERVES 2

HAVE READY: saucepan, grater, measuring jug

1 bunch watercress
1 small onion
2 medium potatoes
¾pt/450ml vegetable stock (or water)

1 bay leaf
freshly ground black pepper
freshly grated nutmeg

Wash the watercress and trim, if necessary.
Dice the onion and chop the potatoes.
Place the potato and onion in a saucepan with the oil and sauté for five minutes, stirring.
Add the trimmed watercress, stock and seasoning and simmer for fifteen minutes, covered.
Liquidize to the required consistency and serve hot or cold.

GREEN PEA SOUP

SERVES 2

HAVE READY: saucepan, measuring jug, liquidizer or food processor.

8oz/225g frozen peas
1 bunch spring onions, chopped
¾pt/450ml vegetable stock

2 tbsp strained Greek yoghurt
1 tbsp chives, chopped
freshly ground black pepper

Boil the peas and chopped spring onions in the stock for about ten minutes.

Transfer to a liquidizer or food processor and blend to the desired texture, adjusting the amount of stock as necessary.

Stir in the yoghurt and chives (leaving some aside) and season to taste.

For the garnish, place a blob of yoghurt on the top with a few chopped chives.

DORIS GRANT'S MUSHROOM SOUP

Doris Grant is the co-author of *Food Combining for Health* in which the Hay system of eating (avoiding protein and starch combinations of food) is explained. Doris is also famous for the Grant loaf and she makes a pretty good mushroom soup too.

SERVES 2–3

HAVE READY: saucepan, measuring jug, liquidizer or food processor, nutmeg grater.

1oz/25g unsalted butter
1 small onion
8oz/225g dark-gilled open
   mushrooms
1 medium-size carrot
1 stick celery
1 heaped tsp yeast extract

1pt/600ml water
freshly grated nutmeg
sea salt
freshly ground black pepper
1 tbsp double cream
paprika (or whipped cream) to
   garnish

Melt the butter in a saucepan, add the onion and cook until pale golden brown.

Add the vegetables, yeast extract and water and bring to the boil. Simmer for fifteen minutes.

Transfer to the liquidizer or food processor and when smooth reheat in the saucepan with a pinch of finely grated nutmeg and season to taste.

Just before serving, stir in the cream.

Garnish with a pinch of paprika (or some whipped cream for special occasions).

PISTOU SOUP

SERVES 2–3

HAVE READY: large saucepan, grater, can-opener.

1½pts/900ml vegetable stock
8oz/225g new potatoes
8oz/225g baby carrots
6oz/175g French beans
4 ripe tomatoes, skinned

14oz/400g can cannellini (or other white beans)
4oz/100g wholemeal pasta shapes
3 tbsp pesto
Parmesan cheese, to serve

Heat the stock.

Dice the potatoes and carrots (which don't need to be peeled but just scrubbed or scraped).

Wash and trim the French beans, then dice.

Add the vegetables to the hot stock, cover and simmer for ten minutes.

Chop the tomatoes and add to the soup with the cannellini beans and the pasta and continue cooking, uncovered, for a further twelve minutes until the pasta is cooked but still *al dente*.

Remove from the heat and stir in the pesto.

Serve at once, offering Parmesan separately.

PASTA SOUP

SERVES 2–3

HAVE READY: large saucepan, can-opener, grater.

1 large onion
1 clove garlic
2 sticks celery
1 tbsp olive oil
14oz/400g can tomatoes
1½pts/900ml vegetable stock

4oz/100g wholemeal pasta shapes
handful freshly chopped parsley
2 carrots, grated
freshly ground black pepper
Parmesan cheese, served separately

Dice the onion, garlic and celery. Place in a saucepan with the oil, cover and cook over a low heat for about ten minutes.

Add the tomatoes and break them up with the back of a wooden spoon.

Add the stock and the pasta and cook for a further twelve minutes.

Remove from the heat and stir in the parsley and freshly grated carrot.

Season with pepper and serve with Parmesan cheese.

WEEK-DAY PUDDINGS

You were probably told as a child that you couldn't have your pudding unless you'd eaten your main course. Now I am about to tell you that you shouldn't have pudding every day. That's because puddings should be for treats and kept for the weekend. However, if you cannot survive without them here are a few suggestions. Basically they are fruit, fruit and fruit . . .

- Fresh fruit
- Fresh fruit salad
- Real fruit yoghurts (see p. 79 for suggestions) or yoghurt poured over raw or stewed fruit (or natural yoghurt with fruit purée stirred in).

A *little*, preferably low-fat, cheese with wholemeal crackers, bread or fruit

Wholemeal pancakes or crêpes (p. 204) filled with fresh sliced fruit, fresh or dried fruit purées

Fruit jelly made with real fruit and fruit juice set with agar agar (Mango Jelly p. 193)

An 'alternative' sorbet or ice-cream (see pp. 71–3)

A fruit 'fool' made with yoghurt and fruit purée

A brûlée made with fresh or thawed frozen fruit, topped with strained Greek yoghurt and grilled with a teaspoonful of Demerara sugar on top

A dried fruit compote

Grilled or baked fruit

Fruit kebabs – strawberries, blueberries, small stoned plums, grapes etc. on satay or small wooden skewers

SPECIAL-OCCASION MENUS

Where cooking can be a chore in the week (now hopefully made a little quicker and easier . . .), it can be a pleasure at the weekend when you are entertaining family or friends.

And here are some menus from countries where vegetarian food is a part of the culture. If your friends are not vegetarian, you can invite them to a Chinese meal or a Thai dinner and you don't even have to mention the word 'vegetarian' (although most people actually like to go out for a vegetarian meal because it is different). And if your friends *are* vegetarian, which is equally likely these days, then you can treat them to something different from the usual old favourites you might have prepared for them before.

Eating food from foreign cultures also means that you can get away from the over-formal restriction of a three-course meal and enjoy the freedom of sampling little tastes of different dishes.

CHINESE DINNER PARTY MENU

A real Chinese meal is a collection of dishes usually served at once, differing from our three-course-meal pattern – although Chinese banquets often have ten courses and more.

Desserts do not feature prominently in Eastern food and they are very unlike our own sweet cakes, pastries and mousses. Often they are made with slightly sweet pulses such as adzuki beans and soyabeans and are very bland to our taste. I have made a Western version of a Chinese-style dessert to give you a taste of the traditional type of dessert, but you could serve oranges, tangerines or an orange-based fruit salad, if preferred.

The spices and pastes used in the recipes are widely available, being made by Sharwoods and sold in supermarkets. But do investigate a Chinese supermarket or food store if you have one near by. You can serve the meal with a China tea, such as Jasmin, made very weak and without milk or sugar. Or you could try a light white wine, such as an Italian or Portuguese. Whether you attempt chopsticks or not is up to you.

181

SERVES 4

Crispy Spiced Cabbage
Mushrooms in Black Bean Sauce
Hot Cashews and Brown Beans
Sweet and Sour Beansprouts

Noodles with Peas
Golden Treasure Rice

Date and Sesame Dessert
or Oranges

CRISPY SPICED CABBAGE

Make six to eight hours before needed.

1 small white cabbage (about
   12oz/325g)

2 tsp five spice mixture
¼pt/150ml brown rice vinegar

Finely slice or shred the cabbage and place in a bowl.
Sprinkle over the spice and the vinegar and cover. Store in the fridge
and turn every couple of hours before serving.

MUSHROOMS IN BLACK BEAN SAUCE

HAVE READY: peeler, grater, saucepan or frying pan, fish-slice
for frying.

8oz/225g large dark mushrooms
1 green pepper
½in/1.75cm root ginger

1 tbsp sesame oil
1 small jar Sharwoods black bean
   sauce

Cut the mushrooms into thickish slices.
Slice the pepper into thin strips.
Peel and grate the ginger.
Add the vegetables to the pan with the oil and sauté for five minutes,
stirring as they cook.
Add the jar of sauce and continue cooking, stirring well, until
completely heated through but leaving the pepper with some
crispness.

HOT CASHEWS AND BROWN BEANS

HAVE READY: food flask or Thermos, garlic press, frying pan,
fish-slice or wooden spoon.

NIGHT BEFORE/MORNING: Soak the dried beans in a food flask or Thermos of boiling water and then boil for forty-five to fifty minutes.

3 chillies
1 clove garlic
¼ tsp chilli powder
1 tbsp sesame oil

4oz/100g whole cashews
8oz/225g cooked brown beans
2 tsp Sharwoods yellow bean paste

Deseed and dice the chillies.
Crush the garlic.
Place them both with the chilli powder and oil in a saucepan and cook over a moderate heat for about three minutes. Do not brown.
Add the nuts, beans and the paste and continue cooking, stirring from time to time, until the mixture has heated through completely.

SWEET AND SOUR BEANSPROUTS

HAVE READY: colander, saucepan.

½ pack beansprouts (about
  4oz/100g)
4 tbsp shoyu sauce
2 tbsp brown rice vinegar

juice of an orange
1 tsp tomato purée
1 dsp Demerara sugar
2 tbsp water

Wash the beansprouts thoroughly in the colander, then drain.
Place the remaining ingredients in a saucepan and heat until the sugar has dissolved.
Add the beansprouts and cook for about two minutes, so that they are hot and still crisp.

NOODLES WITH PEAS

HAVE READY: boiling water, large saucepan.

1 packet of egg noodles (about
  9oz/250g)
6oz/175g peas

4 spring onions
1 vegetable bouillon cube
boiling water

Place the noodles in a saucepan with the peas.
Dice the spring onions finely and add with the bouillon cube to the noodles.

Add twice the volume of boiling water and cook following the manufacturer's instructions – about five minutes.

The liquid should be absorbed but drain, if necessary, before serving.

GOLDEN TREASURE RICE

HAVE READY: food flask or Thermos, can-opener, large saucepan.

NIGHT BEFORE/MORNING: Soak the apricots in a food flask or Thermos of boiling water until swelled and soft.

4oz/100g brown rice	6 apricots (dried), diced
6 dates (fresh or dried), pitted and diced	8oz/225g can water chestnuts, whole or halved

Wash the rice and bring to the boil in twice its volume of water. Cook for about thirty to thirty-five minutes. For the last ten minutes of its cooking, stir in the other ingredients, prepared by soaking (or cooking) and then dicing. Drain.

DATE AND SESAME DESSERT

The Chinese and Japanese have traditional desserts based on soyabeans, tofu and other sweet-tasting beans such as the adzuki. They are works of art, delicately coloured and shaped or sculpted, and look very appetizing, but they are not very sweet to Western tastes. This recipe is very like some traditional desserts but to suit us is slightly sweeter and less bland.

HAVE READY: large and small saucepans, boiling water, lunchbox, liquidizer or food processor.

4oz/100g dates	1 tsp agar agar
10oz/275g tofu	4 tbsp cold water
2 dsp tahini (sesame seed paste)	

Cook the dates in a saucepan with twice their volume of boiling water until soft.

Remove stones and drain, if necessary.

Place the tofu in a liquidizer or food processor and add the dates.

Add the tahini and blend to a purée.

Sprinkle the agar agar on to the cold water in a small saucepan and stir to dissolve over a moderate heat. Blend it into the tofu mixture.

Pour the mixture into a square container such as a small lunchbox and place in the fridge to set for about two to three hours.

To serve, cut into cubes or rectangles and place on a flat plate. Be careful because it is a soft set.

GREEK DINNER PARTY MENU

In Britain, we usually like our food piping hot or chilled and it comes as a surprise at first to discover the Greek preference for foods that are just slightly warm, or at room temperature where we might expect them to be chilled. But on reflection this is sensible as it allows the flavour of the foods to come through better.

Like many other menus from foreign parts, the Greek meal need not necessarily fit a three-course-menu arrangement, although it can lend itself readily to this pattern. Traditionally, there would be extensive *mezze*, common to other near-Eastern countries. These are a selection of dishes such as stuffed vegetables, pâtés and dips, or individual pastries that can be eaten in an informal way or served as a splendid array of dishes in the centre of the table from which everyone helps themselves.

In this menu you can use the Aubergine Pâté as a starter and serve it with warm pitta bread cut into strips. You could also use the Greek Salad as a starter or have it with, or after, the hot dishes. The good thing about Greek food is that it is very versatile and informal while being delicious and surprising. The Greek Garlic Potato dish was first introduced to me by the cookery writer Alkmini Chaitow from Corfu who makes hers with an intoxicating amount of garlic and olive oil which is delicious but might intimidate first-time triers – add more to my recipe if it is to your taste. The dessert is a reduced-sugar form of Baklava which usually has a sugar syrup poured over it. A light brushing of honey can give this sweet taste without drowning in sweetness.

SERVES 4

Aubergine Pâté and
  wholemeal pitta bread

Greek Salad
Stuffed Peppers

| Greek Butter Beans | Rose-water Baklava |
| Garlic Potato | Lemon 'Cream' |

AUBERGINE PÂTÉ

(Microwave and conventional oven)

HAVE READY: lemon squeezer, food processor or blender, serving-dish, fork.

2 large aubergines	1 tbsp tahini (sesame seed paste)
1½ lemons, squeezed	freshly ground black pepper
1 tbsp olive oil	freshly chopped parsley for garnish

Set the oven to 350°F/180°C/Gas 4.

Wipe the aubergines and pierce the skins.
Cook on HIGH for six minutes or until the flesh is soft. Alternatively, bake in a conventional oven for fifty to sixty minutes.
Scrape the flesh from the skins and place in a food processor or blender with the rest of the ingredients. Blend to a purée.
Place in a serving-dish.
Make a pattern on the top with a fork and garnish with parsley.

Serve with warmed wholemeal pitta bread, cut in strips.

GREEK SALAD

6 plum or 4 beefsteak tomatoes	DRESSING
4oz/100g feta cheese (or feta with	4 tbsp olive oil
herbs and garlic)	1 tbsp white wine vinegar
black olives	1 tsp meaux mustard
	1 tbsp lemon juice
	fresh oregano leaves

Slice the tomatoes thickly and arrange them on a serving-dish in rows. Cut the cheese into cubes and sprinkle between the tomatoes. Scatter the olives over the cheese.
Pour the dressing over the top and sprinkle with oregano leaves.

STUFFED PEPPERS
(Microwave and conventional oven)

HAVE READY: lemon-squeezer, garlic press, casserole with lid, saucepan, teaspoon.

3oz/75g brown rice (or 4 heaped
  tablespoonfuls of cooked rice)
2 red peppers
2 green peppers
1 onion
1 clove garlic

½ tbsp olive oil
1½oz/40g pine kernels
1½oz/40g currants
1 tsp ground cinnamon
juice of half a lemon

Set the oven to 350°F/180°C/Gas 4.

Boil the rice in twice its volume of water for twenty minutes.

Cut the tops off the peppers and deseed them. Reserve the tops. Slice a little off the bottoms of the peppers so they will sit evenly in the casserole dish. Place them in the microwave oven, covered, with three tablespoonfuls of water on HIGH for three minutes. Alternatively, you can boil the topped peppers for a minute, if you are not using a microwave oven.

Dice the onion and garlic and sauté in the oil in a saucepan for four minutes. Remove from the heat and stir in the pine kernels, currants, cinnamon and lemon juice.

Drain the rice, if necessary, and stir into the onion mixture.

Stuff the peppers, replace the tops as lids and cook on HIGH for four to five minutes. Or, cook the stuffed peppers in the oven for forty to forty-five minutes, covered, with the addition of four tablespoonfuls of water (or stock) to the dish to prevent it drying out or burning.

GREEK BUTTER BEANS

HAVE READY: food flask or Thermos, saucepan, garlic press, can-opener, heavy-based saucepan with lid, oven-proof casserole.

NIGHT BEFORE/MORNING: Soak the beans in a food flask or Thermos in plenty of boiling water.

8oz/225g butter beans, soaked
1 large onion
2 cloves garlic
3 sticks celery

1 tbsp olive oil
1lb 13oz/800g can tomatoes
sea salt
freshly ground black pepper

Set the oven to 350°F/180°C/Gas 4.

Boil the beans for forty minutes in plenty of water and drain.
Dice the onion, crush the garlic and slice the celery.
Place these vegetables in a saucepan with the oil and sauté for about
fifteen minutes, stirring from time to time.
Add the tomatoes and the beans and cook, covered, for a further
forty minutes.
Or you can transfer the beans to a casserole dish and cook them in the
oven from this stage, if preferred.

GARLIC POTATO

HAVE READY: saucepan, liquidizer or food processor, lemon
squeezer, garlic press, pastry-brush, serving-dish.

NIGHT BEFORE/MORNING: Make the whole dish, as it is
served cold.

1lb/450g potatoes	1 tbsp olive oil for garnish
2 tbsp olive oil	black olives
juice of a lemon	freshly chopped parsley
4 cloves garlic, crushed	

Scrub or peel the potatoes and boil.
Drain and transfer to a liquidizer or food processor.
Add the oil, lemon juice and crushed garlic. Blend to a very smooth
purée.
Transfer to a serving-dish and allow to get cold.
Garnish with a tablespoonful of olive oil brushed over the purée.
Scatter some black olives around the edge of the dish and some
chopped parsley on top.

ROSE-WATER BAKLAVA

HAVE READY: Swiss-roll tin, pastry brush, mixing bowl and
wooden spoon (or electric mixer), wire cooling tray.

4oz/100g soft vegetable margarine
4oz/100g light Muscovado sugar
2 free-range eggs
4oz/100g ground almonds
1oz/25g wholemeal flour

4 drops concentrated rose-water
9 sheets of filo pastry
little sesame oil
sesame seeds (optional)
1 tbsp clear honey

Set the oven to 350°F/180°C/Gas 4.

Cream together the margarine and sugar until light and fluffy.
Beat in the eggs, one at a time.
Fold in the almonds, flour and rose-water.
Lightly oil a Swiss-roll tin and place three sheets of filo pastry (cut to fit) in the base.
Place half the sponge filling on top, levelling as you do so.
Place three sheets of filo on top and then spread the rest of the sponge and level it out.
Top with three sheets of filo, lightly brush with sesame oil and sprinkle over sesame seeds, if liked.
Bake for twenty-five to thirty minutes until golden brown. Protect with greaseproof paper towards the end of cooking if the filo pastry is getting too brown. Or you can discard the top, over-browned layer of filo after baking.
Place on a wire tray to cool and drizzle a tablespoon of clear honey over the top.

LEMON 'CREAM'

HAVE READY: jug or mixing bowl, wooden spoon.

8oz/225g strained Greek yoghurt
juice of half a lemon (or drop of
   lemon oil)

2 tsp cinnamon

Gradually stir the lemon juice into the yoghurt with the cinnamon.
Sprinkle a little extra cinnamon over the 'cream' in its jug or bowl before serving.

INDIAN DINNER PARTY MENU

An Indian meal will not usually follow a pattern of three courses. It is more likely to be a collection of dishes and, in the case of a vegetarian meal, there will be a couple of vegetable dishes and a bean (or other pulse) dish, some rice and/or Indian breads, making a well-balanced protein meal.

The bonus for entertaining with Indian food is that much of it can be made in advance and reheated just before it is needed. Any cold accompaniments such as *raita* (yoghurt and cucumber) and chutneys can be made in advance, too. Another good thing about Indian food is that there is a variety of dishes, so if your guests don't like one thing, they will usually find others they do.

This menu uses rice rather than Indian breads because it is simpler, especially for first-time Indian cooks; the breads take some experience and puffed deep-fried breads such as *poori* have a habit of not puffing when you have guests! (They also add calories and fats.)

Buying individual spices will give much better results than relying on ready-blended curry powders which are much inferior to your own blend of spices. The spices won't be wasted because you will find many other dishes in which to use them.

SERVES 4

Spicy Black-eye Beans
Whole Lentil Dal
Cauliflower with Fennel

Aubergines in Chilli Sauce
Vegetable Pilau

Mango Jelly or Mango Salad

SPICY BLACK-EYE BEANS

HAVE READY: food flask or Thermos, colander, saucepan, heavy-based large saucepan, can-opener, wooden spoon.

NIGHT BEFORE/MORNING: Wash and then soak the beans in plenty of boiling water in a food flask or Thermos.

8oz/225g black-eye beans
2oz/50g okra
1 tbsp cumin seed
1 tsp turmeric

1 tbsp vegetable oil
2 onions, diced
1 green pepper, diced
2, 14oz/400g cans tomatoes

Drain the beans and boil in twice their volume of boiling water for thirty-five minutes.

Wash the okra and dry well. Top and tail and cut into small rounds.
Place the cumin seed and turmeric in a heavy-based deep saucepan
with the oil and add the okra, onion and green pepper.
Cover and sweat for ten minutes, stirring from time to time.
Add the tomatoes and their juice. Break them up with the back of a
spoon as you continue to cook the mixture.
Then add the beans and simmer, uncovered, for a further twenty to
twenty-five minutes.

WHOLE LENTIL DAL

HAVE READY: large saucepan, heavy-based large saucepan,
garlic press, wooden spoon, teaspoon.

8oz/225g whole green continental
  lentils
1 tbsp vegetable oil
2 onions, diced
2 cloves garlic, crushed
1in/2.5cm root ginger, grated

1 tsp each ground cumin, coriander
  and garam masala
½ tsp turmeric
½pt/300ml vegetable stock
8oz/225g frozen spinach

Wash the lentils and pick over to remove the grit or stones.
Place in a saucepan in twice their volume of boiling water and cook
for twenty minutes.
Pour the oil in a heavy-based saucepan and sauté the onion, garlic
and ginger for five minutes, stirring while they cook.
Add the spices as you stir.
Drain the lentils, if necessary, and add to the saucepan of sautéed
vegetables.
Mix thoroughly and add the stock and frozen (or thawed) spinach.
Simmer uncovered for a further fifteen minutes.

Note

I find it easier to buy spinach frozen in nuggets the size of large eggs.
These can be weighed easily when frozen and thaw quickly if added
during cooking to dishes like the above and also to sauces.

CAULIFLOWER WITH FENNEL

HAVE READY: measuring jug, frying pan or saucepan, fish-slice or wooden spoon.

1 large cauliflower
1 tbsp vegetable oil
1 tbsp black mustard seeds

2 tsp fennel seeds
1 tsp garam masala
4–5 tbsp vegetable stock

Wash the cauliflower and break into florets.
Place the oil in a frying pan or saucepan and sauté the mustard and fennel seeds until they are hot and pop.
Add the spice and cauliflower and continue cooking over a low heat for about ten minutes, stirring well.
Add the stock to prevent the cauliflower from sticking or burning.

AUBERGINES IN CHILLI SAUCE

HAVE READY: garlic press, saucepan, wooden spoon, measuring jug.

4 green chillies (or fewer, if preferred)
1in/2.5cm root ginger, grated
2 cloves garlic, crushed
¼ tsp paprika
1 tbsp vegetable oil

8oz/225g tomatoes, chopped
1 onion, diced
1 large aubergine, cubed
1 large potato, cubed
½pt/300ml vegetable stock

Deseed and dice the chillies and place them with the ginger, garlic and paprika in a saucepan with the oil. Sauté for five minutes.
Add the chopped tomatoes, diced onion, cubed aubergine and potato.
Continue cooking and stir to prevent the vegetable mixture sticking.
Add the stock after about five minutes and simmer uncovered for a further thirty. Top up with a little stock, if necessary, but the idea is to reduce the liquid.

VEGETABLE PILAU

HAVE READY: bowl, large saucepan, boiling water, measuring jug.

6oz/175g long-grain brown rice
   (such as Basmati)
4 dried red chillies
1 vegetable stock cube
1 tbsp vegetable oil

½ tsp turmeric
4oz/100g peas, fresh or frozen
2oz/50g okra, sliced
½pt/300ml vegetable stock

Wash the rice well, then transfer it from the bowl to a saucepan with the chillies, stock cube and twice the volume of boiling water.
Boil for twenty minutes, then drain.
Add the oil to the cleaned pan with the turmeric and drained rice. Stir well over a moderate heat to colour the rice.
Add the vegetables and stock and continue to cook for a further fifteen minutes until the liquid is absorbed.

MANGO JELLY

HAVE READY: small saucepan or microwave oven-proof ramekin, terrine or fancy jelly mould.

1 tsp agar agar
4 tbsp cold water
½pt/300ml mango juice

2 mangoes
1 small punnet strawberries
2 pears

Sprinkle the agar agar on to the water in a small saucepan and stir over a moderate heat to dissolve (or sprinkle on to water in a ramekin and cook in the microwave on HIGH for thirty seconds).
Leave to cool, then add the mango juice.
Peel the mangoes and slice.
Hull and halve the strawberries.
Peel and dice the pears.
Place layers of the fruit in the jelly mould or terrine.
Pour the mixed juice and gelatine over the fruit and transfer to the fridge to set.
Cut slices from the terrine and place on individual serving-dishes, or unmould the jelly.

MANGO SALAD

HAVE READY: peeler, serving bowl.

2 ripe mangoes
1 ripe banana
1 pear
1 eating apple

½ pineapple
mango or orange juice
2 tbsp Grand Marnier (optional)

Peel the mangoes and slice the flesh off the stones into a salad bowl. Add the other sliced or chopped fruit and pour over the juice (and liqueur, if liked). Then keep in the fridge until about forty to fifty minutes before needed when it should have come round a little to room temperature (unless it's a boiling hot summer day!).

THAI DINNER PARTY MENU

Having perhaps developed your taste for Chinese food, you might now be branching out into the subtle flavours of Thai food.

Like the Chinese menu, the Thai meal does not really fall into a three-course format but you can serve a salad and perhaps a Satay dip with crudités as a starter and then follow this with a selection of dishes for a savoury menu.

Lemon grass and limes are available in supermarkets which carry a good range of spices and fresh herbs.

Coconut is the predominant flavour in both sweet and savoury cooking and you could offer your guests a choice for dessert between banana and coconut baked custard and coconut cake. Both are made with fresh coconut and are delicious.

Making your own coconut milk is quite a long-winded process but therapeutic, I think, with all the 'working' of the coconut! However, if you prefer, you can take a short cut and grate some creamed coconut and blend it with boiling water.

SERVES 4

Peanut Dip with Crudités
Vegetable Salad

Nutball Satay
Thai Stir-fry
Brown Rice with Lemon Grass
Satay Sauce

Banana and Coconut Pudding
or Coconut Cake

Coconut Milk
or Quick Coconut Milk

PEANUT DIP WITH CRUDITÉS.

HAVE READY: grater, pestle and mortar, garlic press, saucepan.

1in/2.5cm root ginger
2 cloves garlic
2 red chillies
1 tbsp vegetable oil

½oz/12g green peppercorns
2 tbsp crunchy peanut butter
juice of a lemon
¼pt/150ml coconut milk

Grate the ginger. Blend it to a paste in a pestle and mortar with the crushed garlic and finely chopped chillies.
This will bring out the flavours of the spices well.
Put the paste in a saucepan with the hot oil and cook over a low heat, stirring all the time, for two or three minutes.
Stir in the rest of the ingredients and make a thick paste, stirring all the time. Cook for a minute or two, then remove from the heat.
Put in a ramekin and allow to cool and set before serving with prepared crudités.

VEGETABLE SALAD

HAVE READY: wok or frying pan, saucepan, serving-dish.

5–6oz/150–75g tofu, cubed
½ tbsp vegetable oil
2 tbsp shoyu sauce
juice of an orange

8oz/225g new potatoes, small
2 hard-boiled free-range eggs
1 crunchy lettuce (or mixture of
lettuce and radicchio)

Stir-fry the tofu in the oil.
Remove from heat and pat with absorbent kitchen paper to remove excess oil. Toss in the shoyu and orange juice.
Boil the potatoes in their skins, drain and cool.
Peel the eggs and quarter them.
Place the lettuce on a dish and arrange the rest of the salad ingredients on top.

NUTBALL SATAY

HAVE READY: small wooden kebab skewers (cut big ones in half, if necessary), grater.

1 onion, grated
2 chillies, chopped
1 dsp peanut butter
6oz/175g mixed finely chopped
 nuts

2 green peppers
1 red pepper
2 onions

Blend the onion, chillies, peanut butter and mixed nuts to make a firm paste. Form into balls.

Cut the peppers and onions into bite-size pieces that will fit on to the skewers and blanch them. Drain and arrange the nutballs and vegetables alternately on the skewers.

Grill for about fifteen minutes, turning once.

THAI STIR-FRY

HAVE READY: wok or deep saucepan, fish-slice, lime squeezer.

1 tbsp vegetable oil
4oz/100g tofu, cubed
4oz/100g cashew nut pieces,
 toasted
8oz/225g baby sweetcorn

10 spring onions, diced
1in/2.5cm root ginger
1 clove garlic, crushed
juice of two limes

Place the oil in a wok or deep saucepan and heat until hot but not smoking.

Add all the ingredients, except the lime juice, and stir-fry for about seven minutes until cooked and hot but still crunchy.

Pour over the lime juice and toss well, then serve.

BROWN RICE WITH LEMON GRASS

Allow 2oz/50g dry weight of rice per person. Wash, then boil in plenty of water with ½ tsp ground turmeric (or saffron if you are feeling extravagant) and a stick of crushed lemon grass until cooked (or the water is absorbed).

SATAY SAUCE

HAVE READY: pestle and mortar, frying pan or saucepan, wooden spoon, measuring jug, lime-squeezer.

1 stick lemon grass
2 fresh chillies
1 tsp red chilli powder
½ tbsp vegetable oil

2 heaped tbsp crunchy peanut
  butter
6 fl oz/175ml thick coconut milk
1 tbsp Muscovado sugar
juice of two limes

Crush the lemon grass and chillies to a paste in a pestle and mortar with the chilli powder. Sauté in the oil for three minutes, stirring all the time. Add the peanut butter and blend well. Stir in the coconut milk and the sugar. Finally, stir in the lime juice. Do all this over a low heat and, if necessary, thin with a little boiling water, which should also be stirred in over the heat.

BANANA AND COCONUT PUDDING

HAVE READY: measuring jug, saucepan, 8in/20cm-diameter oven-proof dish (lightly oiled), bowl, fork, sieve.

1pt/600ml skimmed milk
2 drops vanilla essence
½ banana

4oz/100g freshly grated coconut
1 tbsp fructose
3 free-range eggs

Set the oven to 350°F/180°C/Gas 4.

Warm the milk and vanilla essence.

Slice the banana into the dish and sprinkle over the coconut and fructose.

Lightly beat the milk into the eggs and through a sieve pour over the dish.

Place in the oven to bake for thirty-five minutes when the custard should be set.

Serve warm or cold but not hot.

COCONUT CAKE

HAVE READY: cake tin (see size in recipe), electric mixer.

3 free-range eggs, separated
3oz/75g soft vegetable margarine
3oz/75g light Muscovado sugar
2oz/50g wholemeal flour

1 tsp baking powder
3oz/75g wholemeal semolina
4oz/100g fresh coconut
4 tbsp skimmed milk

Set the oven to 350°F/180°C/Gas 4.

Lightly oil a 6½ × 6½in/15cm × 15cm-square cake tin.
Whisk the egg-whites in an electric mixer.
Change the attachments and cream the margarine and sugar. Then add the yolks. Sift the flour and baking powder and fold in with the semolina, coconut and milk.
Fold in the whisked egg-whites and place in the cake tin and bake for thirty minutes.
When cooked, sprinkle a little coconut on top. (Don't be tempted to bake the cake with coconut sprinkled over it because if the coconut is fresh it will go an unattractive green colour and if desiccated, will go brown.)

COCONUT MILK

HAVE READY: hand-drill, liquidizer or food processor, sieve, large bowl, measuring jug.

2 coconuts

Makes ¾pt/450ml thick milk and 1pt/600ml thinner milk.
Also produces 8oz/225g flesh per coconut.

Drill a hole in the coconuts, drain off the liquid, chill and use in drinks. A worthwhile cook's perk!

Cut away the brown outer skin and dice the flesh.
Place in a liquidizer or food processor and add a little warm water. Blend for two or three minutes.
Squeeze out to produce a thick milk. Press through a sieve.
Return the flesh to the liquidizer and add ½pt/300ml warm water.
Repeat the pressing and sieving to produce thin coconut milk.
Store in the fridge for up to four days or freeze.

QUICK COCONUT MILK

You can buy a tub or bar of creamed coconut. Grate some into a bowl, then blend with boiling water to achieve the consistency you require – thick or thin.

COOKING AHEAD

These are recipes for when you have more time to spend in the kitchen. They are all for items that can be baked and then frozen for future use in lunchboxes or for lunches/snacks at home (although you won't want to freeze the fruit cake!)

If you do plan to bake and freeze, remember to allow everything to become completely cold before freezing. For ease of use and access, you might like to pack all your breads and bakes ready-sliced, although if stored this way they will dry out more. Slipping a piece of freezer film between the slices will allow you to take them out easily. Even if you forget to defrost them the night before, you can grab a few slices in the morning, which will have defrosted by the time you open your lunchbox (if you have eaten breakfast, that is . . .)

VEGETABLE PASTIES

You can use any seasonal vegetable of your choice to fill the pasties – you will need about 12oz/325g filling.

MAKES 4

HAVE READY: saucepan, mixing bowl, rolling pin, pastry board, 7in/17cm-diameter plate (to cut around), measuring jug, grater.

1 onion
2 potatoes
1 large carrot
4oz/100g mushrooms
⅛ pint/75ml vegetable stock
1 tsp mixed herbs of choice
freshly ground black pepper

FOR THE PASTRY
8oz/225g wholemeal flour
4oz/100g soft vegetable margarine
2oz/50g mature cheddar cheese, grated
1 tsp dry mustard powder
cold water to mix
1 tsp wholemeal flour (for board)
skimmed milk or beaten egg to glaze

Set the oven to 400°F/200°C/Gas 6.

Prepare the vegetables by dicing well and placing in a saucepan with the stock and seasoning. Cover and cook over a low heat for about five minutes while you make the pastry.

Stir them once or twice so they cook evenly. Season to taste.

Sift the flour into a mixing bowl and rub in the margarine until the mixture resembles breadcrumbs in consistency. Stir in the cheese and mustard powder and then mix with cold water to a soft pastry dough.

Roll out on a floured board, cutting out four seven-inch/17cm circles.

Arrange the filling down the centre of the circles and damp the edge of the circle with a little water or skimmed milk.

Draw up the edges and pinch together in a fluted pattern along the seam.

Place on a baking tray and glaze with skimmed milk or beaten egg and bake for twelve minutes. Then turn the oven temperature down to 350°F/180°C/Gas 4 until the vegetables are cooked – about a further twenty minutes.

VEGETABLE SAMOSAS

Samosas can be oily because they are usually deep-fried. This recipe bakes them, so they are crispy but not oily. It also uses wholemeal flour.

MAKES 10

HAVE READY: mixing bowl, jug, garlic press, large saucepan, baking tray, rolling pin, pastry brush.

6oz/175g wholemeal flour
1 tsp baking powder
3oz/75g soft vegetable margarine
cold water to mix

FILLING
2 cloves garlic
2 green chillies
1in/2.5cm piece root ginger
1 tsp ground cumin
1 dsp white mustard seeds

pinch paprika
1 tbs vegetable oil
8oz/225g sweet potato, diced
1 green pepper, diced
1 onion, diced
8oz/225g tomatoes
4oz/100g peas
1oz/25g fresh coriander, chopped
egg-wash for glazing

Set the oven to 200°C/400°F/Gas 6.

Sift the flour and baking powder into a mixing bowl. Rub in the margarine until the mixture resembles breadcrumbs in consistency. Stir in enough cold water to make a soft pastry. Cover while you prepare the filling.

Crush the garlic and finely dice the chillies. Grate the ginger and cook these ingredients, together with the cumin, mustard seed and paprika, in the oil in a covered pan for about five minutes, stirring well. Add the potato, pepper and onion and continue cooking for about five minutes. Roughly chop the tomatoes and add to the pan, together with the peas. Cover and cook slowly for a further ten minutes. Remove from the heat and stir in the coriander. Spread the filling in a shallow dish to cool while you roll out the pastry.

Cut out five 5in/12.5cm circles and cut each in half. Brush the edges of the circles with water or egg-wash. Roll them into cones and place a spoonful of filling in each. Pinch the edges together to seal and place on a baking tray. Glaze with egg-wash and bake for about fifteen minutes until golden brown.

OATCAKES

MAKES 20 OATCAKES

HAVE READY: mixing bowl, saucepan, boiling water, pastry board, rolling pin, palette knife, lightly oiled baking tray.

8oz/225g fine or medium oatmeal	boiling water to mix
2oz/50g wholemeal flour	1 tbsp wholemeal flour (for board)
1 tsp baking powder	little oatmeal as garnish
2oz/50g soft vegetable margarine	

Set the oven to 375°F/190°C/Gas 5.

Mix the oatmeal, flour and baking powder.

Melt the margarine in a saucepan and stir into the dry ingredients.

Gradually, and carefully, add enough boiling water to make a dough. Do not add too much and make it sticky.

Knead very lightly on a floured board until firm enough to roll out into a rectangle.

Trim edges and cut out triangular oatcakes.

Slip palette knife under them and lift on to the prepared or non-stick baking tray.

Sprinkle with a little oatmeal and bake for ten to fifteen minutes.

CRUNCHY BISCUITS

MAKES ABOUT 16 BISCUITS

HAVE READY: mixing bowl, fork, pastry board, rolling pin, biscuit cutter, pastry brush, lightly oiled baking tray, wire cooling tray.

4oz/100g fine oatmeal
2oz/50g wholemeal flour
1oz/25g Demerara sugar
1 tsp baking powder
2½oz/125g soft vegetable
  margarine

1 free-range egg
1 tbsp skimmed milk
milk or beaten egg to glaze
1 tbsp wholemeal flour (for board)

Set the oven to 375°C/190°C/Gas 5.

Mix the oatmeal, flour, sugar and baking powder in a bowl.
Rub in the margarine and then make a well in the centre.
Beat together the egg and milk and mix to a stiff dough.
Roll out on a lightly floured surface and cut out the biscuits with a cutter.
Place the biscuits on the prepared or non-stick baking tray and brush with milk or beaten egg to glaze.
Bake for fifteen minutes until golden brown.
Cool and crisp on a wire cooling tray.

GRANARY CROISSANT ROLLS

MAKES 12 ROLLS

HAVE READY: measuring jug, mixing bowl, clean teatowel, pastry board, rolling pin, pastry brush, baking tray.

½oz/12g fresh yeast
¼pt/150ml lukewarm milk
4 tbsp lukewarm water
1 level tbsp clear honey
4oz/100g unsalted butter
6oz/175g Granary flour

4oz/100g wholemeal flour
2oz/50g melted soft vegetable
  margarine
1 tbsp wholemeal flour (for board)
skimmed milk or beaten egg to
  glaze

Set the oven to 425°F/190°C/Gas 7.

Crumble the yeast into a jug and mix with the milk, water and honey.
Rub the butter into the flour and make a well in the centre.
Mix in the yeast liquid and the melted margarine to form a wet dough.
Cover the bowl with a clean teatowel and leave until doubled in size.
Knock back on a lightly floured board and roll the dough into a large circle. Cut into quarters and then cut each quarter from the centre to the outside edge in three.
Roll up the twelve triangles you have created and bend into crescent shapes.
Transfer to a baking tray and glaze.
Leave to double in size, then glaze again and bake for twenty to twenty-five minutes until golden brown.

CAROB BROWNIES

MAKES 16 BROWNIES

HAVE READY: mixing bowl (or electric food mixer), sieve, lined or greased 7in/17.5cm-square cake tin, wire cooling tray.

4oz/100g soft vegetable margarine	1oz/25g carob powder
2oz/50g Muscovado sugar	3oz/75g walnut pieces
2 free-range eggs	16 walnut halves for decoration
3oz/75g wholemeal flour	2 tbsp jam

Set the oven to 350°F/180°C/Gas 4.

Cream together the margarine and sugar until light and fluffy.
Lightly beat the eggs and blend into the mixture.
Sift the flour and carob powder and fold into the mixture. Then fold in the walnut pieces.
Spoon into a lightly oiled or lined 7in/17.5cm-square baking tin and bake for thirty minutes until an inserted skewer comes out clean.
Transfer to a wire cooling tray and when cold remove from tin. Cut into squares and top each with a walnut half secured with a blob of jam.
Alternatively, you can freeze the brownies at this stage and then decorate once defrosted.

Wholemeal Pancakes

MAKES ABOUT 10 PANCAKES

HAVE READY: mixing bowl, sieve, fork, measuring jug, fish-slice or palette knife, omelette, crêpe or frying pan.

4oz/100g wholemeal flour
pinch sea salt (optional)
1 free-range egg

½pt/300ml skimmed milk
vegetable oil for cooking

Sift the flour into a mixing bowl and add the salt if you are using it.
Lightly beat the egg and make a well in the centre of the flour.
Add the egg and using the fork gradually work in the flour, drawing it from the edge of the well.
Then work in the milk until you have a smooth batter.
To make the pancakes, smear an omelette, crêpe or heavy-based frying pan with vegetable oil.
Heat, but do not over-heat so that the oil smokes.
Pour in enough batter to coat the base of the pan when it is tipped from side to side to spread the mixture.
Cook on one side, then slip a fish-slice or palette knife beneath the pancake and flip it over to cook on the second side.
Cover and keep warm or allow to cool if you are going to freeze the pancakes.

Buckwheat Crêpes

Buckwheat crêpes have a lacy texture and are different in colour to wholemeal pancakes.

MAKES ABOUT 12 CRÊPES

HAVE READY: mixing bowl, sieve, fork, measuring jug, fish slice or palette knife, omelette, crêpe or frying pan.

2 free-range eggs
1 tbsp sunflower oil
3fl oz/90ml cider or beer

4oz/100g buckwheat flour
6fl oz/180ml water
vegetable oil for cooking

Lightly beat together the eggs, oil and cider or beer.
Sift the flour, then add the liquid gradually, whisking all the time with a fork to form a smooth batter.
Gradually thin with water and whisk again.
Leave to stand for ten minutes.
Make the crêpes in the usual way (see above, Wholemeal Pancakes).

RICH FRUIT BREAD

This is a yeasted fruit bread that can be made in a couple of small bread tins or in a fancy mould such as a savarin. If you haven't used yeast before, don't be put off, it's quite straightforward.

HAVE READY: measuring jug, saucepan, sieve, mixing bowl, fork, clean teatowel, pastry board, two lightly oiled 1lb/450g bread tins or a savarin mould.

1oz/25g fresh yeast	1lb/450g wholemeal flour, sieved
¼pt/150ml warm water	4oz/100g raisins
3oz/75g soft vegetable margarine	2oz/50g mixed peel
¼pt/150ml skimmed milk	4oz/100g walnut pieces
2oz/50g clear honey	2 tbsp wholemeal flour (for board)
2 free-range eggs	

Set the oven to 400°F/200°C/Gas 6.

Crumble the yeast into the water and leave to stand.
Melt the margarine and warm the milk.
Add the margarine, milk, honey and lightly beaten eggs to the yeast.
Sift the flour and place half in a bowl.
Pour on the liquid, beat in and then cover the wettish dough with a clean teatowel.
Leave to rise for thirty minutes.
Beat in the rest of the flour, the dried fruits and nuts. Lightly knead on a floured board.
Place in the tins (or savarin) and cover again until well risen (about two thirds up the sides of the tins).
Bake for forty minutes.
Cool a little before removing from the tins (or savarin).

DIGESTIVE BISCUITS

Finding digestives without animal fat was difficult in the past but there are some brands available now (see p. 38). However, digestives are still a nice biscuit to bake and, if you are still hooked on biscuits, they are one type that has fewer calories and less fat and sugar than most others.

MAKES ABOUT 14 BISCUITS

HAVE READY: sieve, mixing bowl, measuring jug, fork, rolling pin, pastry board, pastry cutter, lightly oiled baking tray, wire cooling tray.

3oz/75g wholemeal flour
1oz/25g fine oatmeal
pinch sea salt
1½oz/40g soft vegetable margarine

½ tbsp Demerara sugar
2½–3fl oz/60–75ml water
1 tsp wholemeal flour (for board)

Set the oven to 350°F/180°C/Gas 4.

Sift the flour into a mixing bowl and stir in the oatmeal and salt.
Rub in the margarine and stir in the sugar.
Bind to a soft dough with the water.
Roll out on a lightly floured board.
Cut out, using 2½in/6cm cutters.
Place on the baking sheet and bake for twenty to twenty-five minutes.
Cool on a wire tray to crisp before storing in an airtight tin or freezing.

SULTANA SCONES

Another favourite standby for teatime, lunch or evenings.

MAKES 12 SCONES

HAVE READY: sieve, mixing bowl, measuring jug, lemon squeezer, fork, pastry board, pastry cutter, pastry brush, rolling pin, lightly oiled baking sheet.

8oz/225g wholemeal flour
1 tsp baking powder

2oz/50g soft vegetable margarine
2oz/50g sultanas

2 tsp lemon juice
¼pt/150ml skimmed milk
2oz/50g Demerara or Muscovado
  sugar

1 tsp wholemeal flour (for board)
skimmed milk to glaze

Set the oven to 425°F/220°C/Gas 7.

Sift the flour and baking powder into a bowl.
Rub in the margarine and stir in the sultanas and sugar.
Make a well in the centre of the dry ingredients.
Add the lemon juice to the milk and pour into the well, stirring with a fork to form a soft dough.
Turn on to a floured surface and roll out to about ¾in/2cm thickness. Cut out twelve scones with a pastry cutter.
Transfer to the baking sheet and glaze.
Bake for fifteen minutes or until an inserted skewer comes out clean.

Note

You can make these scones without sugar, especially if you spread them with jam or honey. However, some people will miss the sweet taste, so you can compensate by adding a teaspoonful of mixed spice or cinnamon (or other sweet spice of your choice).

Cheese Scones

The same basic ingredients and method can be used as above but instead of stirring in sultanas and sugar, add 4oz/100g grated mature cheddar-style cheese and a pinch of cayenne pepper or dry mustard.

MALT LOAF

This is not as sticky as the shop-bought varieties but is usually well received.

CUTS INTO 10 SLICES

HAVE READY: saucepan or oven-proof microwave, dish, sieve, measuring jug, lightly oiled 1lb/450g bread tin.

1oz/25g soft vegetable margarine
2 tbsp molasses
3 tbsp malt barley syrup (Cookie malt or malt extract)

¼ pt/150ml skimmed milk
8oz/225g wholemeal flour
2 tsp baking powder
4oz/100g large seedless raisins

Set the oven to 350°F/180°C/Gas 4.

Place the margarine, molasses, malt and milk in a saucepan over a low heat (or in a dish in the microwave) and dissolve together.
Sift the flour and baking powder into a mixing bowl and stir in the raisins.
Add the liquid and mix thoroughly before spooning into the pre-pared tin and baking for fifty minutes or until an inserted skewer comes out clean.
Cool on a wire cooling tray.

CORN BREAD

A South American speciality which is good served warm with bean dishes and other vegetarian savouries.

HAVE READY: fork, mixing bowl, sieve, measuring jug, lightly oiled 1lb/450g bread tin, pastry brush.

1 free-range egg	2½oz/62g wholemeal flour
4fl oz/120ml skimmed milk	1 tsp baking powder
4½oz/112g cornmeal (maize flour)	

Set the oven to 400°F/200°C/Gas 6.

Lightly beat the egg with the milk.
Sift the cornmeal and flour into a mixing bowl with the baking powder.
Make a well in the flour and gradually beat in the liquid.
Place in the prepared tin and bake for thirty minutes or until an inserted skewer comes out cleanly and the bread is risen and golden.

DATE AND WALNUT BREAD

MAKES 8 SLICES

HAVE READY: mixing bowl, sieve, wooden spoon, lightly oiled 1lb/450g bread tin.

2oz/50g soft vegetable margarine
2oz/50g Muscovado sugar
2oz/50g cooking dates

2oz/50g walnut pieces
1 free-range egg
4oz/100g wholemeal flour

Set the oven to 350°F/180°C/Gas 4.

Cream together the margarine and sugar until light and fluffy.
Chop up the dates and walnuts and add to the mixture.
Lightly beat the egg and blend into the mixture.
Sift the flour and fold into the mixture, together with the bran from the sieve.
Place in the prepared bread tin and smooth the top.
Bake for thirty minutes or until an inserted skewer comes out cleanly.

BANANA BREAD

MAKES 10 SLICES

HAVE READY: mixing bowl, basin, fork, wooden spoon, sieve, grater, lightly oiled 1lb/450g bread tin.

2oz/50g soft vegetable margarine
2oz/50g Muscovado sugar
1 ripe banana (about
    4–5oz/100–150g)

2 free-range eggs
1 carrot
1oz/25g mixed nuts, finely chopped
4oz/100g wholemeal flour

Set the oven to 350°F/180°C/Gas 4.

Cream together the margarine and sugar.
Mash the banana and mix in.
Lightly beat the eggs and add one at a time, adding a little flour in between if the mixture curdles.
Grate the carrot and stir in together with the nuts.
Sift the flour and fold in, including the bran from the sieve.
Place in the prepared tin and bake for thirty-five to forty minutes or until an inserted skewer comes out cleanly.

FLAPJACK

HAVE READY: saucepan, lightly oiled Swiss roll or square baking tin, wire cooling tray.

4oz/100g soft vegetable margarine	2oz/50g golden syrup
1oz/25g Demerara sugar	8oz/225g rolled oats

Set the oven to 350°F/180°C/Gas 4.

Melt the margarine, sugar and syrup together in a saucepan over a moderate heat.
Remove and stir in the oats.
Press into a lightly oiled Swiss roll tin or square baking tin about 7in/17.5cm × 7in/17.5 cm.
Bake for thirty to thirty-five minutes until golden brown and firm.
Remove and cut fingers or squares immediately.
Do not try to remove from the tin until cold when the fingers/squares will have to be re-cut.

FRUIT CAKE

HAVE READY: mixing bowl, wooden spoon, sieve, 8in/20cm cake tin, greaseproof paper, pastry bowl, scissors, skewer.

4oz/100g soft margarine	3oz/75g raisins
2½oz/65g light Muscovado sugar	3oz/75g currants
3 free-range eggs	8oz/225g wholemeal flour
1 tbsp mincemeat	1 tsp mixed spice
1oz/25g pecans, chopped	1 tbsp brandy
1oz/25g flaked almonds	few drops natural almond essence

Set the oven to 300°F/150°C/Gas 2.

Line the cake tin with greaseproof paper, cut to fit.
Beat together the margarine and sugar until light and fluffy, then beat in the eggs, one at a time, adding a little flour if the mixture curdles.
Add the mincemeat, nuts and fruit and stir well.
Sift the flour and mixed spice and fold into the mixture.
Then add the brandy and almond essence.
Place the mixture in the tin, and smooth the top. Cook for thirty minutes, then lower the heat to 275°F/135°C/Gas 1 and cook for 2¼–2½ hours until an inserted skewer comes out cleanly. (Cover the cake with greaseproof paper towards the end of cooking to prevent it over-browning.)

CHEESE BAPS

MAKES 6 BAPS

HAVE READY: sieve, mixing bowl, rolling pin, pastry cutter, baking tray, teatowel.

8oz/225g wholemeal flour
½oz/12g fresh yeast
¼pt/150ml warm water
25mg vitamin C tablet, crushed

skimmed milk for glazing, if liked
3oz/75g red Leicester or Cheddar cheese

Set the oven to 400°F/200°C/Gas 6.

Sift the flour into a mixing bowl.
Mix the yeast with the water and the crushed vitamin C tablet.
Pour the yeast mixture into the flour and mix well to a soft dough.
Knead for five minutes.
Roll out the dough and cut out rounds with a 3in/7.5cm pastry cutter and place on a baking tray.
Cover with a clean teatowel and leave until doubled in size.
Brush the top of the baps with a little skimmed milk, then sprinkle the cheese over.
Bake for twenty minutes.

WHOLEMEAL PIZZA BASES

The recipe below makes two bases which can be frozen for later use or used in recipes such as Presto Pizza (p. 116).

HAVE READY: sieve, mixing bowl, measuring jug, rolling pin.

12oz/325g wholemeal flour
½pt/300ml warm water

½oz/12g fresh yeast
25mg vitamin C tablet

Sift the flour. Crumble the yeast into the water and stir in the crushed vitamin C tablet. Pour on to the flour and work to a soft dough. Knead for about four minutes or mix in an electric mixer. Roll out into two circles and place on a firm surface. Wrap well to store in the freezer.

USEFUL ADDRESSES

The Vegetarian Society
Parkdale
Dunham Road
Altrincham
Cheshire W A 14 4 Q G

(061 928 0793)

The Vegetarian Society
53 Marloes Road
Kensington
London W 8

(01 937 7739)

The Vegan Society
Secretary
47 Highlands Road
Leatherhead
Surrey

Henry Doubleday Research Association
Ryton on Dunsmore
Coventry C V 8 3 L G

(0203 303517)

(For information about organic growing and site of the National Organic Gardening Centre)

The Soil Association
86 Colston Street
Bristol B S 1 5 B R

(0272 290661)

(For information about organic growing)

INDEX

FOR THE BEST IN PAPERBACKS, LOOK FOR THE 🐧

In every corner of the world, on every subject under the sun, Penguin represents quality and variety – the very best in publishing today.

For complete information about books available from Penguin – including Pelicans, Puffins, Peregrines and Penguin Classics – and how to order them, write to us at the appropriate address below. Please note that for copyright reasons the selection of books varies from country to country.

FOR THE BEST IN PAPERBACKS, LOOK FOR THE 🐧

COOKERY IN PENGUINS

Jane Grigson's Vegetable Book   Jane Grigson

The ideal guide to the cooking of everything from artichoke to yams, written with her usual charm and depth of knowledge by 'the most engaging food writer to emerge during the last few years' – *The Times*

More Easy Cooking for One or Two   Louise Davies

This charming book, full of ideas and easy recipes, offers even the novice cook good wholesome food with the minimum of effort.

The Cuisine of the Rose   Mireille Johnston

Classic French cooking from Burgundy and Lyonnais, including the most succulent dishes of meat and fish bathed in pungent sauces of wine and herbs.

Good Food from Your Freezer   Helge Rubinstein and Sheila Bush

Using a freezer saves endless time and trouble and cuts your food bills dramatically; this book will enable you to cook just as well – perhaps even better – with a freezer as without.

An Invitation to Indian Cooking   Madhur Jaffrey

A witty, practical and delightful handbook of Indian cookery by the much loved presenter of the successful television series.

Budget Gourmet   Geraldene Holt

Plan carefully, shop wisely and cook well to produce first-rate food at minimal expense. It's as easy as pie!

Mediterranean Food   Elizabeth David

Based on a collection of recipes made when the author lived in France, Italy, the Greek Islands and Egypt, this was the first book by Britain's greatest cookery writer.

The Vegetarian Epicure   Anna Thomas

Mouthwatering recipes for soups, breads, vegetable dishes, salads and desserts that any meat-eater or vegetarian will find hard to resist.

A Book of Latin American Cooking   Elisabeth Lambert Ortiz

Anyone who thinks Latin American food offers nothing but *tacos* and *tortillas* will enjoy the subtle marriages of texture and flavour celebrated in this marvellous guide to one of the world's most colourful *cuisines*.

Quick Cook   Beryl Downing

For victims of the twentieth century, this book provides some astonishing gourmet meals – all cooked in under thirty minutes.

Josceline Dimbleby's Book of Puddings, Desserts and Savouries

'Full of the most delicious and novel ideas for every type of pudding' – *Lady*

Chinese Food   Kenneth Lo

A popular step-by-step guide to the whole range of delights offered by Chinese cookery and the fascinating philosophy behind it.

COOKERY IN PENGUINS

The Beginner's Cookery Book   Betty Falk

Revised and updated, this book is for aspiring cooks of all ages who want to make appetizing and interesting meals without too much fuss. With an emphasis on healthy eating, this is the ideal starting point for would-be cooks.

The Pleasure of Vegetables   Elisabeth Ayrton

'Every dish in this beautifully written book seems possible to make and gorgeous to eat' – *Good Housekeeping*

French Provincial Cooking   Elizabeth David

'One could cook for a lifetime on this book alone' – *Observer*

Jane Grigson's Fruit Book

Fruit is colourful, refreshing and life-enhancing; this book shows how it can also be absolutely delicious in meringues or compotes, soups or pies.

A Taste of American Food   Clare Walker

Far from being just a junk food culture, American cuisine is the most diverse in the world. Swedish, Jewish, Creole and countless other kinds of food have been adapted to the new environment; this book gives some of the most delicious recipes.

Leaves from Our Tuscan Kitchen   Janet Ross and Michael Waterfield

A revised and updated version of a great cookery classic, this splendid book contains some of the most unusual and tasty vegetable recipes in the world.

PENGUIN HEALTH

Audrey Eyton's F-Plus   Audrey Eyton

'Your short-cut to the most sensational diet of the century' – *Daily Express*

Caring Well for an Older Person   Muir Gray and Heather McKenzie

Wide-ranging and practical, with a list of useful addresses and contacts, this book will prove invaluable for anyone professionally concerned with the elderly or with an elderly relative to care for.

Baby and Child   Penelope Leach

A beautifully illustrated and comprehensive handbook on the first five years of life. 'It stands head and shoulders above anything else available at the moment' – Mary Kenny in the *Spectator*

Woman's Experience of Sex   Sheila Kitzinger

Fully illustrated with photographs and line drawings, this book explores the riches of women's sexuality at every stage of life. 'A book which any mother could confidently pass on to her daughter – and her partner too' – *Sunday Times*

Food Additives   Erik Millstone

Eat, drink and be worried? Erik Millstone's hard-hitting book contains powerful evidence about the massive risks being taken with the health of consumers. It takes the lid off the food we eat and takes the lid off the food industry.

Pregnancy and Diet   Rachel Holme

It *is* possible to eat well and healthily when pregnant while avoiding excessive calories; this book, with suggested foods, a sample diet-plan of menus and advice on nutrition, shows how.

PENGUIN HEALTH

Medicines: A Guide for Everybody   Peter Parish

This sixth edition of a comprehensive survey of all the medicines available over the counter or on prescription offers clear guidance for the ordinary reader as well as invaluable information for those involved in health care.

Pregnancy and Childbirth   Sheila Kitzinger

A complete and up-to-date guide to physical and emotional preparation for pregnancy – a must for all prospective parents.

The Penguin Encyclopaedia of Nutrition   John Yudkin

This book cuts through all the myths about food and diets to present the real facts clearly and simply. 'Everyone should buy one' – *Nutrition News and Notes*

The Parents' A to Z   Penelope Leach

For anyone with a child of 6 months, 6 years or 16 years, this guide to all the little problems involved in their health, growth and happiness will prove reassuring and helpful.

Jane Fonda's Workout Book

Help yourself to better looks, superb fitness and a whole new approach to health and beauty with this world-famous and fully illustrated programme of diet and exercise advice.

Alternative Medicine   Andrew Stanway

Dr Stanway provides an objective and practical guide to thirty-two alternative forms of therapy – from Acupuncture and the Alexander Technique to Macrobiotics and Yoga.

PENGUIN HEALTH

A Complete Guide to Therapy   Joel Kovel

The options open to anyone seeking psychiatric help are both numerous and confusing. Dr Kovel cuts through the many myths and misunderstandings surrounding today's therapy and explores the pros and cons of various types of therapies.

Pregnancy   Dr Jonathan Scher and Carol Dix

Containing the most up-to-date information on pregnancy – the effects of stress, sexual intercourse, drugs, diet, late maternity and genetic disorders – this book is an invaluable and reassuring guide for prospective parents.

Yoga   Ernest Wood

'It has been asked whether in yoga there is something for everybody. The answer is "yes" ' – Ernest Wood.

Depression   Ross Mitchell

Depression is one of the most common contemporary problems. But what exactly do we mean by the term? In this invaluable book Ross Mitchell looks at depression as a mood, as an experience, as an attitude to life and as an illness.

Vogue Natural Health and Beauty   Bronwen Meredith

Health foods, yoga, spas, recipes, natural remedies and beauty preparations are all included in this superb, fully illustrated guide and companion to the bestselling *Vogue Body and Beauty Book*.

Care of the Dying   Richard Lamerton

It is never true that 'nothing more can be done' for the dying. This book shows us how to face death without pain, with humanity, with dignity and in peace.

GARDENING IN PENGUINS

The Penguin Book of Basic Gardening   Alan Gemmell

From the perfect lawn to the flourishing vegetable patch: what to grow, when to grow and how to grow it. Given the garden, a beginner can begin on the day he buys this book with its all-the-year-round Gardener's Calendar.

The Pip Book   Keith Mossman

All you need is a pip and patience . . . 'The perfect present for the young enthusiast, *The Pip Book* should ensure that even the most reluctant avocado puts down roots and sends up shoots' – *The Times*

The Town Gardener's Companion   Felicity Bryan

The definitive book for gardeners restricted by the dimensions of their gardens but unrestrained by their enthusiasm. 'A fertile source of ideas for turning a cat-ridden concrete backyard into a jungle of soothing green' – *Sunday Times*

Water Gardening   Philip Swindells

A comprehensive guide to the pleasures and uses of expanses of water, however great or small in the garden. Includes advice on aquatic and marginal plants and the management of ornamental fish.

Beat Garden Pests and Diseases   Stefan Buczacki

An invaluable book, covering all types of plants, from seedlings to root vegetables . . . there is even a section on the special problems of greenhouses.

The Englishman's Garden   Alvide Lees-Milne and Rosemary Verey

An entrancing guided tour through thirty-two of the most beautiful individual gardens in England. Each garden is lovingly described by its owner. Lavishly illustrated.

GARDENING IN PENGUINS

A History of British Gardening   Miles Hadfield

The great classic of gardening history. 'One of the most interesting, stimulating and comprehensive books to have come my way. It should be on every gardener's bookshelf . . . a remarkable book' – Cyril Connolly in the *Sunday Times*.

Roses for English Gardens   Gertrude Jekyll and Edward Mawley

Illustrated with beautiful photographs, this book demonstrates the nearly limitless possibilities for planting the best-loved flower of all – between walls, on pergolas, along wood posts, on verandas, and on trees.

Labour-Saving Gardening   Tom Wright

At last, a guide to make sure that you get maximum pleasure from your garden – with the least effort and just a little forethought and planning. Every aspect of gardening is investigated – all to save your most precious commodities: your energy and your time.

Gardens of a Golden Afternoon   Jane Brown

'A Lutyens house with a Jekyll garden' was an Edwardian catch-phrase denoting excellence, something fabulous in both scale and detail. Together they created over 100 gardens, and in this magnificent book Jane Brown tells the story of their unusual and abundantly creative partnership.

Window Boxes and Pots   Martyn Rix

Patio, balcony or windowsill – all can be transformed into an eye-catching delight with this wonderfully informative guide. Whether you settle for lobelia cascading from a hanging basket or geraniums of white, soft pink and cosy scarlet, you can be sure that Martyn Rix will tell you all you need to know.

FOR THE BEST IN PAPERBACKS, LOOK FOR THE

A CHOICE OF PENGUINS

Castaway Lucy Irvine

'Writer seeks "wife" for a year on a tropical island.' This is the extraordinary, candid, sometimes shocking account of what happened when Lucy Irvine answered the advertisement, and found herself embroiled in what was not exactly a desert island dream. 'Fascinating' – *Daily Mail*

Out of Africa Karen Blixen (Isak Dinesen)

After the failure of her coffee-farm in Kenya, where she lived from 1913 to 1931, Karen Blixen went home to Denmark and wrote this unforgettable account of her experiences. 'No reader can put the book down without some share in the author's poignant farewell to her farm' – *Observer*

The Lisle Letters Edited by Muriel St Clare Byrne

An intimate, immediate and wholly fascinating picture of a family in the reign of Henry VIII. 'Remarkable . . . we can really hear the people of early Tudor England talking' – Keith Thomas in the *Sunday Times*. 'One of the most extraordinary works to be published this century' – J. H. Plumb

In My Wildest Dreams Leslie Thomas

The autobiography of Leslie Thomas, author of *The Magic Army* and *The Dearest and the Best*. From Barnardo boy to original virgin soldier, from apprentice journalist to famous novelist, it is an amazing story. 'Hugely enjoyable' – *Daily Express*

India: The Siege Within M. J. Akbar

'A thoughtful and well-researched history of the conflict, 2,500 years old, between centralizing and separatist forces in the sub-continent. And remarkably, for a work of this kind, it's concise, elegantly written and entertaining' – Zareer Masani in the *New Statesman*

The Winning Streak Walter Goldsmith and David Clutterbuck

Marks and Spencer, Saatchi and Saatchi, United Biscuits, G.E.C. . . . The U.K.'s top companies reveal their formulas for success, in an important and stimulating book that no British manager can afford to ignore.